rüffer & rub visionaries

Hans R. Herren

HOW TO
NOURISH
THE
WORLD

Translated by Sue Coles

The author and publisher wish to thank the
Elisabeth Jenny Foundation for its generous support.

rüffer&rub Sachbuchverlag is supported by the
Federal Office of Culture, Switzerland, from 2016 to 2020.

Originally published as *So ernähren wir die Welt*
Copyright © 2016 by rüffer & rub Sachbuchverlag GmbH, Zurich

First edition Spring 2017
Copyright © 2017 by rüffer & rub Sachbuchverlag GmbH, Zurich
info@ruefferundrub.ch | www.ruefferundrub.ch

Typeface: Filo Pro
Printing and binding: Books on Demand GmbH, Norderstedt
Paper: Cream white, 90 g/m²

ISBN 978-3-906304-25-0

Foreword [by Anne Rüffer] 6

A world without hunger and misery 8

1. Surfeit of hunger 11

2. Threats to resources 19

3. Risks of climate change 27

4. My vision 30

5. How can we achieve our goal? 33

6. A new lifestyle 55

7. IAASTD Report and its consequences 60

My vision in practice 65

Marimanti, Kenya: The holy mountain

      is turning green again 66

Push-Pull keeps pests and weeds in check 70

Bhutan: Target: 100% organic 76

SACDEP, Kenya: Open field days for organic farming 80

Meru, Kenya: Mangoes are no longer crying 86

Meru, Kenya: Making a living with indigenous varieties ... 94

Women carry the burden of responsibility 98

Towelo, Tanzania: Mountain carrot 104

Using biochar to protect the climate and soils 108

Farmer Communication Programme for East Africa 116

Rice: Production boost thanks to the

      System of Rice Intensification 124

Appendix 126

Biovision 127

Notes 132

List of photos and diagrams 143

About the author 143

Foreword

Geneva, 2 December 2015: A large and distinguished audience had assembled in the Ivan Pictet Auditorium to honour the latest winners of the Right Livelihood Award, widely referred to as the "Alternative Nobel Prize". Rarely has the address of the venue so matched the event itself as the "Maison de la Paix" is hosting the event opened by Germany's Minister of the Environment Barbara Hendriks and the UN Director General Michael Møller entitled "On the Frontlines and in the Courtrooms: Forging Human Security".

In the subsequent discussion involving the four laureates, there is one statement that electrifies me. "The UN was founded after the Second World War in order to protect future generations from being hostage to war. Since then there have been more than 170 conflicts and was there never an opportunity to discuss the elimination of war? Come on guys—that's just not credible!" Embarrassed laughter and sheer amazement in the audience even though Dr Gino Strada, founder of the international aid organisation Emergency knows only too well what he is talking about. Since the early 1990s, he has built clinics in war zones and looked after civilian victims—only 10% were fighters from the warring factions, the other 90% were civilian. He ended by saying: "Feel free to call me a utopian; everything is a utopia until somebody implements it."

One of the most quoted sentences of recent decades is "I have a dream." Not only Martin Luther King had a dream—many of us dream of a fairer world for all and a few—more than you might think—realise their dream with commitment and with all their heart and mind. They are pioneers in their field; you may call people such as Gino Strada, Martin Luther King, Mother Teresa or Jody Williams utopians but each great achievement starts with an idea, a hope, a vision.

Our new series—we call it "rüffer&rub visionary"—sets out to pass on this glimmer of an idea, a hope, a vision and so ignite the spark of personal commitment. At its heart is the author's personal dialogue with a particular issue. Each tells an enthralling story of how they became aware of a scientific, cultural or social issue and what prompted them to search for robust answers and sustainable solutions. The writers all display great commitment. They describe what it means to make a personal commitment to pursue and to live an idea. Whether the vision is political, scientific or spiritual, all of the authors have one thing in common; they yearn for a better world and are prepared to work with all their strength to achieve it.

The issues and activities may be extremely diverse, but common to all visionaries is that they act from a deep conviction that a better future for all on a healthy planet is possible. We are convinced that everyone of us can, through our own actions, be a part of the solution.

Anne Rüffer, publisher

A world without
hunger and misery

My vision of a sustainable food system for the world goes back a long way. I am a farmer's son. My father was estate manager for the Domaine des Barges in Switzerland's Lower Valais that was owned by the Burger und Söhne (Aargau) tobacco dynasty. The 40-hectare farm grew tobacco, potatoes and wheat.

I experienced intensive farming at first hand: it meant spraying highly poisonous insecticide to control the caterpillars of the diurnal and nocturnal moths that feasted on the tobacco leaves. It was the use of fungicides to control imported fungal diseases. They not only destroyed the pests but also eliminated beneficial insects such as bees. When I was growing up I found it quite normal, even though occasionally I also wondered whether so much poison was actually good for humans or the environment. At the time, we knew no different and it seemed as though chemicals were an essential ingredient of modern agriculture.

I spent two winters and a summer as a student at Valais Agricultural College in Châteauneuf learning what farmers needed to know about crops and fruit growing, vineyards and livestock management, i.e. that the use of agrochemicals guaranteed good harvests and a better life.

Having matriculated with a baccalaureate, I embarked in 1969 on an agronomy degree at the Swiss Federal Institute of Technology (ETH) in Zurich, with plant protection as my main subject and plant breeding as my subsidiary. At ETH plant protection almost exclusively, with one exception, meant the use of chemical methods to control damaging insects, weeds and fungi.

It was the era of the "Green Revolution", the term used to describe the development that started in the 1960s of modern, high-performing and high-yielding crop varieties and their successful spread throughout developing countries. As a young ETH student I was seriously impressed by the higher yields that could be achieved with high-performing varieties and the massive application of agrochemicals. At the same time, however, I started to look critically at this type of agriculture and question it.

My doctoral supervisor, "the one exception", was Vittorio Delucchi, a professor of entomology. He was a pioneer in Switzerland for integrated and biological pest management, promoting the use of natural enemies and agronomic practices rather than synthetic insecticides to control pests. Entomologists had long known that you could control pests if you could find their natural enemies, i.e. the corresponding beneficial insects. However, it seemed too complicated and expensive for the conventional agricultural industry to find these beneficials, breed them in sufficiently large numbers for commercial use and to find a suitable way to release them into the fields—despite the fact that it had been known for a long time that the method worked.

Vittorio Delucchi gave me an introduction to the research group of Robert van den Bosch at the University of California in Berkeley, which at the time was the mecca for entomologists in the field of biological pest control. In 1979, whilst at the International Institute for Tropical Agriculture (IITA) in Ibadan, Nigeria, I had an opportunity to put into practice my knowledge of the biological control of the mealybug—a pest that devastated the cassava crops.[1]

I remained in Africa for 27 years working in the field of biological pest control. This experience and the knowledge I gained made me realize that fundamental changes were needed to agriculture—in fact to the entire global food system.

It is an ambitious aim: a world free from hunger and misery, where everyone enjoys the same right to live in freedom with one another and in harmony with nature. A world where the boundaries of Planet Earth are respected and violence and war are outlawed. Where the needs of future generations are at the very top of the political agenda; natural resources are regenerated and preserved on their behalf. A world where energy supplies are based 100% on renewable energy sources.

In this vision, the food system plays a crucial role.

1. Surfeit of hunger

One in nine people go to bed hungry. According to a report on food security published in 2015 by the FAO, the UN Food and Agricultural Organisation, 795 million people—just under 11% of the global population—are malnourished. Although the figure has fallen by 216 billion since the beginning of the 1990s,[2] it fails by some margin—more than half a billion—to achieve the goal set by the World Food Summit in 1996 to halve the absolute number of people without enough food between 1990 and 2015.

One in seven children under five years of age is underweight. Malnutrition contributes to the deaths of 3.1 million children under five each year—that is more than 45% of all deaths in this age group.[3] Africa, south of the Sahara, is the worst-affected region with 23% of the population currently malnourished; in the Caribbean it is slightly under 20%.[4]

Some two billion people are deficient in vitamins and essential minerals such as iodine and iron, even though they consume enough carbohydrates and protein. This is partly a result of reductions in food diversity; monoculture systems are used to grow essential foodstuffs, which means that certain highly nutritional plants are absent from local diets. Similarly, those living in rich countries are often malnourished because they eat high-calorie processed foods that are low in micronutrients.

Hunger is the greatest risk to global health. However, the reverse is also a problem: a total of 1.4 billion adults in the world are overweight and of these 500 million are obese.[5] Excess weight is a major cause of diabetes, high blood pressure, strokes and many cancers. In 1980, obesity was already affecting one-quarter of all adults and by 2008, that figure had risen to more than one-third; increasingly it is also affecting developing countries and overall, about 50% of the global population eats too little, too much or the wrong type of food.[6]

For many countries in the global South, hunger is a major obstacle to development. It is also a difficult one to overcome: If people have too little to eat, their productivity remains low and hungry children often miss school. It is also costly to treat the associated diseases. A study conducted in several African countries estimated that the cost of hunger in these countries is between 2% and 16% of Gross National Product.[7]

A food system that puts both too much and too little healthy food on the table cannot be a model for the future. The following sections look in more detail at the various issues and demonstrate why the aim of the World Food Summit—to eradicate hunger—has so far been impossible to achieve.

Waste

At present, farmers produce enough food to feed more than 14 billion people; that is twice current global requirements. Unfortunately, not all food ends up being eaten by consumers. According to a study published in early 2003 by the British Institution of Mechanical Engineers, 30–50% of food intended for human consumption is lost.[8] The main reason for this in developing countries is a lack of storage, processing and transport facilities.

The situation is different in industrialised countries. For example, in Switzerland domestic households account for 45% of the loss.[9] Special offers tempt shoppers to buy more than they can consume. In addition, expiry dates are calculated in such a way that perfectly good food is often discarded.

Globally, about one-third of all food produced is currently not consumed. This causes not only a serious economic loss (US\$ 940 billion per year) but also 8% of all greenhouse gas emissions. A study by Porter, Reay, Higgins and Bomberg from the University of Edinburgh found that the loss and waste of food accounted for 2.2 gigatonnes of CO_2 equivalents each year, which is 323 kg CO_2 per person and three times higher than 50 years ago.

Champions 12.3, a coalition of more than 36 business and government representatives as well as those from civil society, published a report during the process leading up to the agreement on the Sustainable Development Goals (SDGs) in autumn 2015. It provided a progress report on the fight against food waste and loss. Although the international community had made considerable efforts to achieve SDG Target 12.3, the report concluded that they were not enough to rectify current deficiencies in the supply chain, including production, delivery and the end consumer.

The report highlighted three particular benefits of eliminating food loss and waste: better food security, lower costs throughout the entire supply chain and finally better protection for resources and the climate. The report called for stakeholders to agree on concrete reduction targets without delay. Progress must be monitored regularly and there must be no ifs and buts. There are already some examples of good practice: Italy and France have both passed legislation to reduce food waste. Instead of dumping edible foodstuffs, supermarkets are now allowed to donate them. Similarly, the United States has announced plans to halve food waste by 2030.

The concern remains, however, that action on Target 12.3 will be limited to a few countries and will only involve larger companies. In addition, the mechanisms for monitoring progress are still inadequate in many areas. The report identified a lack of professional systems and methods for the systematic recording of data that is capable of identifying problem areas. To sum up: if we are to achieve SDG Target 12.3 by 2030, each and every country, town, company and in particular each and every consumer on Planet Earth must show greater commitment to efforts to fight food waste and loss.[10]

Too much meat

Another form of food waste is the high level of meat consumption. To produce one calorie of food from livestock farming requires between two and seven times as much feed as that needed to produce plant-based calories. Global meat consumption has increased fourfold in the last 50 years[11] and the average global consumption per head per year is now 32 kg[12]. In Switzerland it is 51 kg,[13] in Germany 60 kg[14] and in France 86 kg[15]. Although meat consumption has stagnated and in some cases even declined slightly in industrialised countries, it is rising in emerging nations, sometimes very rapidly.

Meat is increasingly produced on an industrial scale in intensive livestock units. This type of farming requires a much greater use of antibiotics. Livestock farming now accounts for 70% of the global use of antibiotics.[16] Excessive use of antibiotics encourages the development of resistance and it is estimated that some 25,000 people die each year in Europe from infections caused by pathogens resistant to antibiotics.[17]

In order to use resources as efficiently as possible, it makes absolute sense for humans to include some animal products in their diet. About two-thirds of the world's available farmland is only suitable for grass or pasture.[18] Ruminants eat grass and so are not competing with humans for food; animals also provide manure and some, like hens and pigs, can eat food waste and by-products—a good sow will eat anything.

However, many animals are fed primarily on cereal and other arable crops: animals currently consume about one-third of current global cereal production.[19] In addition, much of the feed used in meat production in industrialised countries is imported; some 35 million hectares of arable land in the EU is "outsourced" in this way.[20] That means that more than one-third of all EU arable land is not available in developing countries for domestic food production.[21]

The driver behind such misguided trends in livestock farming is the economic pressure to produce as much meat as possible and as efficiently as possible. For those of us living in rich industrialised countries, this makes meat ridiculously cheap; it is also now affordable for the growing middle classes in developing countries, but the poor come away empty-handed. They are still unable to afford meat and livestock farming consumes their plant-based food. According to calculations by UNEP, the United Nations Environment Programme, the calories lost in the process to transform plant matter into animal feed would meet the food needs of 3.5 billion people.[22] It should also be noted that cheap meat is in fact expensive, given that the externalities accruing from the intensive, industrial production and the health impact of excess consumption of such meat are being socialised—and carried by all taxpayers.

Too poor to have enough to eat

More than one billion people live in extreme poverty and have to survive on less than US$ 1.25 per day.[23] Poor families in developing countries spend 50–80% of their income on food;[24]

even a small increase in food prices can threaten their very existence.

For example, weather-related crop failures in 2007 and 2008 increased the demand for renewable raw materials and meat and this, combined with speculative trading, triggered an increase in the price of basic foodstuffs. The FAO Food Price Index rose by 52% in one year from July 2007 to July 2008.[25] As a direct consequence, the number of people suffering from malnutrition increased from 70 million to 100 million. It caused hunger riots in some countries, and it even caused the government to fall in Haiti.

Apparent paradox: Food is too cheap

The problem, however, is not that food prices are too high but rather the reverse. Food is too cheap. To explain this apparent paradox, we need a little background.

The maxim adopted by the agriculture industry is to maximise production, minimise product costs and minimise labour costs. This reductionist approach, geared as it is to maximum yields, requires mechanized production and monoculture systems that favour high-yielding crop varieties. It requires vast amounts of mineral fertilisers, pesticides and water. This in turn overexploits non-renewable natural resources.

In terms of production volumes, this approach has been extremely successful. Even though the global population more than doubled between 1961 and 2011, grain production per capita increased by 30% in the same period. This increase in yields was accompanied by a fall in prices.[26] According to the Swiss Federal Office for Statistics, the average household in Switzerland currently spends just 6.4% of its gross income on food and alcohol-free drinks;[27] in Germany it is 10.5%.[28]

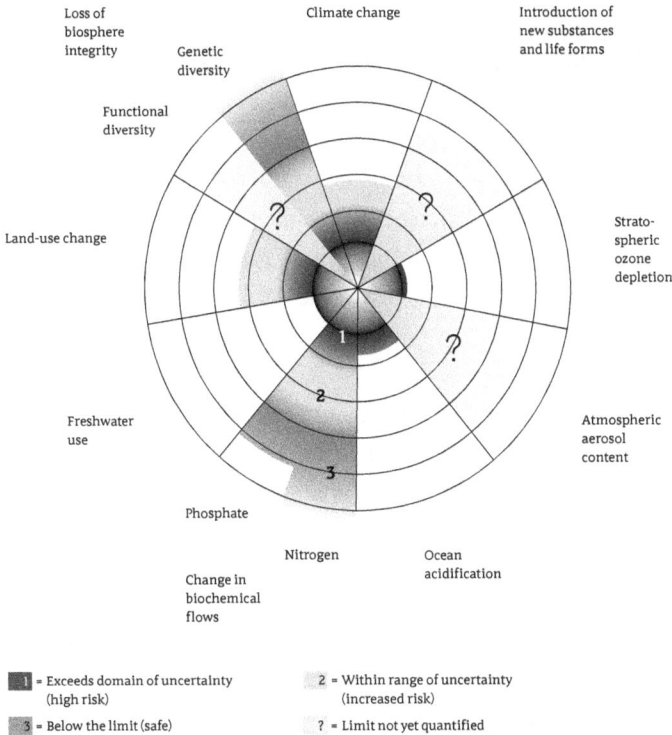

Diagram 1 | "We are reaching the boundaries of Planet Earth." As a result of human influence, the planet has already crossed four of its nine boundaries: climate change, biodiversity, land use and biogeochemical cycles.

Loss of biosphere integrity

Climate change

Introduction of new substances and life forms

Genetic diversity

Functional diversity

Land-use change

Strato- spheric ozone depletion

Freshwater use

Atmospheric aerosol content

Phosphate

Nitrogen

Ocean acidification

Change in biochemical flows

1 = Exceeds domain of uncertainty (high risk)

2 = Within range of uncertainty (increased risk)

3 = Below the limit (safe)

? = Limit not yet quantified

However, only a minority of farmers benefit from new agricultural technology—only those who can afford it. For the vast majority of small-scale farmers in developing countries, a production system that requires huge amounts of expensive high-yielding crop varieties and agrochemicals is not a viable way to increase production and escape poverty.

At the same time, countries from the rich North use export subsidies worth billions of dollars to sell off their surplus produce to those in the South. These imported goods compete with local produce. As a result, more than 70% of those without enough food live in rural areas.[29] Smallholders, farm labourers and landless workers rely directly on agriculture. If the weather is favourable, the harvests are good. They may then have enough to eat but still have little opportunity to earn an income from surplus produce. If the weather is poor, the harvest does not provide enough food, nor do they have money with which to buy food. As a last resort, they migrate to towns, mostly ending up in urban slums. Once there, they rely on cheap and subsidized imports from the rich North for food; these same imports also deny domestic smallholders the opportunity to earn an income.

The problem is exacerbated by the agricultural policies of some countries in Asia, Africa and Latin America. Production for domestic purposes is neglected and the traditional crops needed for a healthy diet are abandoned. Latin America currently produces three times more food than it consumes,[30] whilst at the same time the continent has 34 million people without enough food.[31] Two-thirds of developing countries are either net importers of food or dependent upon food aid from the global North.[32] This form of food system is misguided and further widens the gap between rich and poor, both internationally and within countries. This in turn perpetuates the problem of hunger. The reductionist solutions inherent in industrial agriculture are not only unsuitable but also counterproductive for escaping from this vicious circle. In order to combat poverty, we need a holistic approach; it requires policies on development, trade, social issues and tax that target this objective both internationally and domestically in individual countries. The change to a sustainable food system of the type that I envisage would make a significant contribution towards that objective.

Agricultural land degradation

Between now and 2050, the global population will rise from 7.4 billion to more than 9 billion.[33] The highest growth is likely to be in Africa south of the Sahara, the region currently worst affected by hunger; here the population will more or less double—at a time when agricultural resources are shrinking.[34] Some 5 billion hectares are currently available for farming: 1.5 billion hectares of arable and permanent crops and 3.5 billion hectares of grassland and pasture.[35]

The opportunities to increase the amount of land available for agriculture are limited and any expansion is likely to be detrimental to forests and wetlands. Globally, 60% of forest clearance is done to create farmland.[36] One-third of current farmland is already degraded—to a greater or lesser extent—by erosion, salination, compaction, acidification or pollution.[37] Some 10 billion hectares of land are lost to erosion each year because of inappropriate land use—almost ten times the total agricultural land in Switzerland.[38] New residential developments are gobbling up more and more agricultural land in developing countries. In both cases, it is often the best agricultural land that is lost.

Land grabbing

When it comes to soil, the battle for scarce resources has already begun. Rich oil states, emerging nations such as China and South Korea and increasingly private fund companies from the developed North are buying land in developing countries or leasing it on a long-term basis.

In October 2009 GRAIN, a non-governmental organisation specialising in this issue, listed a total of 140 hedge funds, private equity groups and financial organisations involved in this type of investment.[39] Huge tracts of land are being turned over to monocultures for the production of food, animal feed and agro-fuels intended for export, including in countries where people are suffering from malnutrition. According to estimates by the World Bank, the Sudan leased or sold almost 4 million hectares of land to foreign investors between 2004 and 2009—roughly the total land area of Switzerland.[40] The Land Matrix organisation keeps a record of all land sales and leasehold transactions and its data shows that the global figure currently exceeds 44 million hectares.[41]

Water shortages

About 20% of current arable fields are irrigated and 40% of all food is grown on irrigated land.[42] The huge investment in irrigation systems since the 1950s has played a major role in increasing yields. By 1990, the total area under irrigation had almost tripled and currently 70% of the world's fresh water consumption is used for agriculture.[43]

Water is an increasingly scarce resource in food production. A total of 1.6 billion people live in areas that suffer from water shortages.[44] In many parts of Asia and Africa, the overexploitation of water resources is now a problem in its own right, with groundwater levels dropping rapidly. Water shortages have also reached alarming proportions in the industrial grain-growing belt of the US Midwest.[45]

Loss of biodiversity

Similarly, the biological basis of food production is now much more fragile. Over the millennia, humans have used more than 10,000 plants as crops; today it is just 150 and the few plants still in use are becoming increasingly alike. A total of 12 varieties make up 80% of the plants used for food production.[46]

In the past, farmers have used plant propagation and livestock breeding to produce an enormous range of varieties suitable for use in an extremely wide range of conditions. Not only is the number of varieties shrinking but at the same time we are witnessing the triumphant global march of fewer but higher yielding varieties. For example, the potato is currently the fourth most important staple food and could play an even greater role in future in fighting global hunger. Potatoes were originally grown some 8000 years ago by the indigenous peoples of South America in the Peruvian/Bolivian Andes around Lake Titicaca at altitudes up to 4300 m. In addition to the wild varieties, there are more than 3000 cultivated varieties of potatoes.[47] It is essential that they are protected because it is estimated that 75% of all varieties in the world are no longer cultivated.[48]

Similarly, the biological basis of livestock farming is shrinking just as fast. Since 1900, some 1000 livestock breeds have become extinct—including the Frutigen cow and sheep, the Freiburg cow and the Galloway pony.[49] According to data from FAO, the UN Food and Agricultural Organisation, 1458 breeds, including the Brazilian Pantanerio cow and the Hungarian Mangalica pig, also called the woolly pig, are threatened with extinction; their loss would represent some 17% of all livestock breeds.[50] This development is the result of indiscriminate crossbreeding, the use of non-native species, the decline of traditional forms of production and the neglect of species not deemed sufficiently productive. If the sole aim of agriculture is to maximise output, valuable characteristics are lost, e.g. an animal's ability to withstand heat or cold or to make do with less water or lower quality feed.

Crops and livestock are but two of the factors in food security. In order to introduce new characteristics into crops, we need to make use of related wild varieties. This has been done, for example with millet, where a disease pathogen known as the barley yellow dwarf virus has caused enormous damage. The only way to fight the virus is prompt intervention with an insecticide that kills off the vector. That could soon change. Plant researchers have discovered a gene resistant to the virus in barley living in the wild (*Hordeum bulbosum*) and commonly found in the Mediterranean and Central Asia. This gene has been transferred to cultivated barley (*Hordeum vulgare*) by crossbreeding. The result is a new variety with a resistance to the pathogen.[51]

Hordeum bulbosum is a crop wild relative, or CWR. This is the specialist term used for wild plants that are sufficiently closely related to cultivated plants that their genes are interchangeable. This makes them potentially an excellent source for the breeding of new varieties.

There are more CWRs than you might think. Research has shown that the term can be applied to 83% of all flora in Switzerland and 143 varieties have already been placed on a priority CWR list because of their potential for use in cultivation.[52]

The world's genetic reservoir is being eroded and between 10,000 and 25,000 animal and plant species die out each year.[53] The process of evolution is such that some species will naturally disappear. However, the current rate of extinction is a thousand times faster than the natural rate.[54] Agriculture—directly and indirectly (through deforestation)—is one of the main contributors to the biodiversity crisis.

A diverse animal kingdom is also an insurance against pests. Pests have natural adversaries, i.e. insects that predate or parasitize them. However, the decline in species affects both the beneficial insects and the pests; 35% of global food plants depend upon insects for pollination.[55] More than 100,000 species have a role in increasing harvests. It is currently unclear whether they will be able to perform that function in future. Their populations are being weakened by habitat loss and reductions in crop diversity, as well as by pesticides-neonics in particular—both as topical sprays and as seed coating, mostly on genetically modified organisms (GMOs).

Pesticides in the environment

Recent studies have shown that 11–24% of pollen and 17–65% of nectar from fields sprayed with the insecticide neonicotinoid are contaminated with the poison.[56] This group of insecticides represents a huge threat to the survival of pollinators.

A British study has produced similar findings. It compared data on the distribution of 62 species of wild bees with data on oilseed rape fields sprayed with neonicotinoids. Oilseed rape was chosen because it is attractive to bees. It was found that the pesticide caused significant damage to wild bee populations.[57]

Drift, run-off and leaching cause pesticides to migrate to other habitats and damage their biotic communities. An analysis of 838 studies from 73 countries showed that more than 50% of insecticide concentrations found in surface water exceeded the damage threshold for aquatic organisms.[58]

Between 2005 and 2012, the Swiss canton-based laboratories responsible for water pollution investigated more than 500 watercourses for traces of 203 active agents used as insecticides in agriculture. In 80% of cases, they found active agents and in 50% of cases there was at least one instance when levels exceeded 0.1 μg/l, the legal limit for water pollutants in Switzerland.[59] It should also be remembered that the cumulative effect of pollutants below this level is not necessarily harmless.

Pesticides also pose a risk to agricultural workers. The World Health Organisation (WHO) estimates that between two and five million people are poisoned each year; 40,000 of these cases are fatal.[60] The causes are often the use of highly poisonous substances long since banned in most industrial countries as well as the lack of the necessary protective clothing for farmers in developing countries.

Pesticides also affect consumers. Various studies have linked pesticide residues in food and the environment to chronic disease. In particular, pesticides are suspected of playing a role in the development of cancer, Alzheimer's, birth defects, Parkinson's and some development disorders.[61]

The Environmental Institute in Munich recently examined 14 types of beer available in Germany for the presence of glyphosates. Residues were found in every single case at levels of between 0.46 and 29.7 μg/litre;[62] the limit for drinking water is 0.1 μg/litre.[63] Glyphosate is suspected of being carcinogenic and those demanding a Europe-wide ban are becoming increasingly vocal. In October 2016, the Monsanto Tribunal in The Hague looked at the decade-long use of agrochemicals produced by the company and known to be harmful.[64] It clearly demonstrated that their use has caused immense damage to human health and ecosystems. In addition, the manufacturing processes for agrochemicals (e.g. pesticides and fertilisers) and the monocultures required by their use are playing a significant role in climate change. The business models adopted by Monsanto and other corporations currently dictate global agricultural practices. The best way to promote and introduce agro-ecological methods on a global scale would be to deprive these corporations of the basis of those models. If food were produced in accordance with sustainable principles, we would eventually have no need to use contaminants. We know that they are highly suspect, but they are still produced in large quantities. This would not only avoid damage to the environment but would also benefit the world in other ways, e.g. in terms of health and climate change.

Greenhouse gases from agriculture

Intensive farming is also a driving force behind climate change. It is directly responsible for 13% of greenhouse gas emissions measured in CO_2 equivalents, i.e. methane from the stomachs and intestines of ruminants, nitrous oxide from too many fertilisers and CO_2 from fossil fuels used for energy. A further 18% is produced when forests are cleared to create new farmland.[65] In the last 20 years, greenhouse gases from agriculture have increased annually by 1%, and by far the biggest contributor has been intensive livestock farming.[66]

In addition, the production of mineral fertilisers and agrochemicals as well as the use of agricultural machinery demand vast amounts of energy; this makes farming heavily reliant on fossil fuels. Producing a single food calorie can require up to 10 calories of external energy.[67]

In the final analysis, the ecological problems created by agriculture are the result of a reductionist approach to food production, where the sole aim is to produce as much as possible for as little as possible. However, food is only cheap for the consumer because the system outsources ecological costs, e.g. water pollution from pesticides, soil degradation, loss of biodiversity and the effect on climate change. It is we and our descendants who will end up paying those costs in some form or other.

In the meantime, the maximum yield policy is coming up against biological limits. In recent years, the increase in the yield per hectare from intensive farming has flattened out and between 1950 and 2001, the global rise in yields per year declined from 3% to 1%.[68] In 24-39% of the areas that grow maize, rice, wheat and soya, yields per hectare have recently stagnated or even dropped.[69] Plants cannot indefinitely increase their ability to absorb nutrients and convert them into vegetable material. We should also attach greater importance to quality and nutritional value and less on a process that simply increases the number of "empty" calories so familiar to us since the Green Revolution. It is also part of a new paradigm which was clearly advocated in the International Assessment of Agricultural Science and Technology for Development Report (IAASTD), published in 2008.

This report, compiled by 400 scientists from around the world over a period of four years, came to the clear conclusion that we could only nourish the world sustainably if we refocused our efforts and worked with nature rather than against it. The report, which was initiated by the World Bank and the United Nations, was signed by 58 nations. Unfortunately, however, its proposals have not been implemented.

The Earth is getting warmer; we cannot prevent it even if we were able to reduce greenhouse gases quickly and significantly. The world will suffer more climate-related events, such as too high or too low rainfall, as well as appreciable changes in the overall water balance. Pests and disease pathogens in animals and plants will shift their area of distribution. Each of these problems will present food production with new challenges that will be difficult to overcome.

According to the latest status report from the Intergovernmental Panel on Climate Change (IPCC), there is likely to be a decline in the production of wheat, maize and rice in both tropical and temperate zones if temperatures rise by 2°C compared with levels at the start of the century.[70] This will be particularly true where rainfall levels are also dropping.

The IPCC estimates that unless action is taken to tackle climate change global temperatures will increase by 4°C and sea levels will rise by 0.7 metres by the end of the century—compared in each case with the period 1986–2005.[71] Moreover, there is already some evidence that the IPCC prognoses are somewhat optimistic.

The estimates for rising temperatures are based on assumptions for the climate sensitivity of the Earth's atmosphere. For example, by how much will temperatures increase if the CO_2 content doubles? A study by the British Apollo-Gaia Project looking at climate dynamics concluded that, based on data on the reaction of the atmosphere to past changes in CO_2, the climate is likely to be 2.5 times more sensitive than the IPCC assumptions.[72] If this is true, we can expect much faster and much greater increases in temperature.

Fatal consequences for Africa

Africa is already experiencing the pain of climate change. During the 20th century, temperatures on the African continent rose on average by half a degree. The increase in East Africa was even greater. A review of individual datasets from measuring stations in Kenya, Uganda, Rwanda and Burundi showed an increase of 1.54°C just between 1966 and 2006.[73]

This rise in temperatures has been accompanied by an increase in extreme weather conditions. In the last 25 years, weather-related disasters, e.g. flooding and drought, have doubled.[74] In 2006 devastating floods affected Somalia, Ethiopia, Kenya and Tanzania,[75] and in 2011/12 East Africa experienced its worst drought in 60 years.[76]

According to the IPCC estimates, temperatures in Africa will rise by a further 1.5–4°C by 2100—depending upon the emission scenario used.[77] This warming of the atmosphere will be accompanied by drastic changes in levels of precipitation. Simulation modelling by the Climate Service Center (CSC) has predicted that winter rainfall in South and North Africa will decline by 20%, whereas the increase over an entire year is likely to be almost 10% in East Africa.[78]

Some 90% of agriculture production in Africa depends upon rainfall and is therefore at particular risk from declining precipitation. Conversely, increases can also be a problem because the pattern is likely to be heavier and more frequent rainfall. This in turn will cause flooding and destroy harvests.

Africa is bearing the greatest burden of climate change even though it has contributed next to nothing to the causes.

This was the outcome of a recent a report by Maplecroft, a British company specializing in risk analyses: According to the report, 32 countries are at particular risk of serious damage from climate change; almost all of them are in Africa and South Asia.[79]

The IPCC predicts that drought or heavy rainfall is likely to cause serious production losses as early as 2030–2040. The predictions for the longer term are based on two different scenarios. In the more optimistic case, the world manages to reduce emissions sufficiently to ensure that by 2080 temperatures are only 2°C higher than pre-industrialisation levels—the declared objective of international climate policy. The risks to agriculture in Africa would still remain high but could be reduced to tolerable levels if action were taken to adapt to the new climatic conditions. In contrast, the second scenario's assumption is that if average temperatures were to rise by 4°C, the impact on agriculture would be catastrophic and action taken to adapt to the change would achieve little or nothing.[80]

4. My vision

Diversity not uniformity

By focussing exclusively on maximum output, industrial agriculture is not only reductionist but also lacks basic diversity. It adopts the same standardised model everywhere: monocultures and factory farms dominate the agriculture landscape, and irrespective of where you are in the world, you find the same high-yielding varieties growing in fields maltreated with the same agrochemicals. Industrial agriculture not only damages the environment but insidiously destroys the basis of production. In the final analysis, this uniform system is both fragile and less resilient.

I contrast this model with the diversity offered by the agroecological approach. By this I mean not only the presence of a diverse range of species and varieties on farms but also diverse methods of cultivation. Agroecology is not a standardised concept; it covers a wide range of agricultural systems that are adapted to prevailing conditions and further refined to meet local needs. Common to all of these systems is the principle of ecological, economic and social sustainability in the framework of the food system as a whole.

My vision for agriculture is one that
- does not always strive for maximum yields, but rather seeks yields that are sustainable in the longer term. It is multifunctional: it preserves soils and water supplies, regenerates and retains natural soil fertility, and encourages biodiversity.

- looks after the landscape so that nature can provide its full range of ecological services. It enhances the resilience of the entire production system.
- allows farmers to earn enough money to live on. It pays them a fair price for their produce and a reasonable recompense for their work to protect the environment, nature and the climate.
- protects jobs in rural areas—both directly and indirectly— by providing local processing facilities, thus helping to combat poverty. It offers young people a future in rural areas and halts the exodus to towns.
- provides a sink for CO_2 rather than emits greenhouse gases.
- dispenses with agrochemicals. To maintain yields it uses natural methods to keep pests and weeds in check. It grows a diverse range of crops and combines arable and livestock farming. It seeks closed material cycles.
- adopts production methods that make efficient use of resources such as water. It abandons fossil fuels and minimises food losses.
- is modern. It uses machinery where appropriate and takes advantage of knowledge-intensive systems. It is underpinned by existing traditional knowledge, which is combined with the results of cutting-edge research. Agricultural science seeks to improve its understanding of nature rather than exploit it. It makes use of nature's bounties for the benefit of all, including nature itself.
- produces food mainly where it will be consumed. Local markets offer nourishing, wholesome and affordable foods and so improve the health of local people.
- contributes to an equitable system that supplies those living in rich countries with more plant- and less animal-based produce.

The Earth's natural resources are finite; humans must live on the interest from those resources rather than consuming the capital. We are currently consuming the capital, and by each August we have used up the interest for the entire year. For the rest of the year we consume capital. With each passing year, the date on which we use up that interest advances by one week.

The average ecological footprint per head of population is currently 1.5 times higher than it should be; in the EU it is 2.1 times higher and in Switzerland 3.3 times higher.[81] In essence, we have built our prosperity on a system that is plundering the Earth's natural resources. We must accept that we need nature and give up the notion that technology can make us independent of it. We have developed technical solutions for food production, yet most oft these solutions have already been "invented" by nature. Why take this circuitous route when we could trust nature from the outset? Why not act as though we were a part of nature rather than treating it as our servant?

The problems inherent in current food systems are linked to other problems, such as environmental destruction, economic crises, growing inequality, the social impact of globalization, climate change, health crises, war, violence and terror None of these problems can be solved in isolation; they require a holistic approach.

In an era dominated by aggressive nationalism, the relentless pursuit of profit, intolerance, economic uncertainty and the erosion of international institutions, it may seem utopian to put forward a vision that demands foresight, global cooperation and a willingness to accept the concept of sufficiency. Yet if you really believe in something, you can move mountains.

5. How can we achieve our goal?

My vision is not some utopian ideal. It is quite achievable with current technology or by developing the potential of current technology. What we need, however, is a fundamental change in agricultural policy and a reorientation of agricultural research. A transformation of the food system is not without a cost, but money invested now will avoid much higher costs for future generations. It is an investment in the future.

Encourage small-scale farms

More than 80% of all farms (537 million) have less than 2 hectares of land.[82] Small-scale farmers produce 70% of food on less than 50% of farmland.[83]

From a global perspective, small-scale farms are by far the world's largest employer. A total of 2.6 billion people—40% of the global population—earn their living from them.[84] Whereas agriculture in the industrialised North only makes a small contribution to the gross national product (in Switzerland only 1%),[85] in 20 developing countries the figure exceeds 30%, and 17 of these countries are in Africa.[86]

Numerous studies have shown that small-scale farms deliver a higher yield per hectare and are more productive than large farms. They use fewer technical and chemical aids but more labour.

Small-scale, diverse farming structures are the best way to deliver a sustainable food system—socially, economically and ecologically. I do not seek to romanticize the current traditional farm. Nor am I advocating a return to pre-industrial conditions. We are all too familiar with the sometimes low productivity and efficiency, farming practices that are harmful to health and the environment, and a lack of knowledge; all of these factors contribute to the misery of many small-scale farmers and their families. To meet future demands, we need to focus on innovation and equip farmers with the right skills.

Improved methods of cultivation, the use of appropriate technology, traditional and state-of-the-art knowledge, and a range of agro-ecological strategies have the potential to boost productivity. In addition, investment in small-scale farming is the best way to ensure that higher food production is available where it is actually needed.

Fair prices for producers

Farmers must be paid a fair price for their produce; otherwise they have no incentive to produce more than they need for their own consumption. Instead of seeking to drive down prices, we should be improving living standards. This will allow people to buy good food at a fair price. Investment in small-scale farming is an efficient way to achieve this. The World Bank estimates that economic growth in the agriculture sector is twice as effective at reducing poverty as growth in any other sector.[87]

Food prices must also be fair on the environment, i.e. they must include external costs. The Economics of Ecosystems and Biodiversity (TEEB), an initiative of the UN Environment Programme (UNEP), is currently working on a project to calculate external costs. An initial analysis of global beef production showed that it costs US$170 to produce one kilogram of beef protein if external costs, such as greenhouse gas emissions, conversion of forest into farmland and air pollution are included.[88]

According to a study by FiBL, the Swiss Research Institute of Organic Agriculture, the price paid by consumers would have to increase by about one-third if the external costs of food production were included.[89]

We need to dig deeper into our purse for food. Paying the true cost of food would be an investment in the future. It would reduce the burden on our children and grandchildren, who in any case will have to deal with the consequences of our lifestyles.

Develop rural infrastructure

Healthcare, schools and energy supplies in rural areas must be expanded. There is also a need to develop a processing industry for agricultural produce that creates jobs and increases purchasing power. It is unacceptable to drive a further two billion people from rural into urban areas.

Without adequate road, rail and communication networks, agricultural products cannot reach markets. The the power of multinational agro-businesses is a further major obstacle, and in certain sectors and regions they control the entire supply chain from farm to fork. They thwart efforts to make it easier for small-scale farmers to access markets and in so doing strengthen their own position. Without a strong local market, it is almost impossible to escape the spiral of hunger and poverty or produce enough food for those living in developing countries.

In terms of finance for farmers, microloans can provide them with the required capital, e.g. to invest in suitable machinery or improve soils.

Finally, small-scale farmers need security. They need protection against the risk of production losses and sales guarantees for their produce. In particular, however, they need legal certainty in respect to their right to use the land and other natural resources. Many areas are in urgent need of land reforms so that it is distributed more fairly. Fertile land is increasingly being sold to foreign investors; this undermines efforts to fight poverty and strengthen small-scale agriculture. The soil is a central element of food production and must remain in the hands of local people.

Strengthen the status of women in farming

Women play a major role in food production. They account for between 20% and 70% of those involved in farming and post-harvest activities, and in many developing countries the trend is upwards. Men may well dominate society, but it is women who have the practical skills and do the actual work. If you want to understand how small-scale farming works in Africa and other developing countries or how to improve it, ask the women involved.

Women pay a high price for their efforts, particularly in developing countries. Agriculture involves hard physical labour, including carrying water and wood. This makes women prone to sickness. They also start work when still very young, and thus often miss out on schooling and lack the required skills. Finally, economic and social power remains with men and most women earn little despite their enormous workload. Not only do women earn less but they have fewer rights than their male counterparts. In sub-Saharan Africa, women produce 80–90% of all food but own just 2% of the land. Women are only granted 10% of the microloans for agriculture.[90] It is imperative, therefore, to improve the status of women in agriculture in developing countries. It has been estimated that if women in Africa had equal access to education and agricultural resources, yields would increase by 20–30% and the number of those going hungry would drop by 100–150 million.[91]

Governments must be persuaded to enable women—and also young people—to obtain a good education and ensure that they have access to the results of the latest agricultural research. Their land rights must be strengthened and they must be able to source small loans. Above all, women must receive a fair reward for their labours.

Ecological farming

Ecological farming (agroecology) is not just a luxury for the rich but is essential for our survival. It is the only way to put food production on a sustainable course and safeguard it for future generations. If we are to tackle climate change, global agriculture must switch to an ecological system. This will not only make food production more robust and more resistant but also help to provide a defence against the negative effects of global warming. Ecological farming can also help to limit climate change itself.

It is argued that ecological farming intensifies the pressure on forests and other natural habitats because yields per hectare (acre) are lower and so more land is needed for the same yield. However, this misses the point. In reality, there is little difference in the yields from organic and conventional agriculture. According to a meta-analysis carried out in 2007, yields per hectare from organic farming in industrial countries are 92% of the levels from conventional farming.[92]

It is true that output would fall if all farmland in industrialised countries was converted to organic farming, but that fall would be within acceptable limits. In contrast, on small-scale farms in developing countries—exactly where higher yields are needed—the potential for ecological methods is huge. The United Nations Conference on Trade and Development (UNCTAD) and the UN Food and Agricultural Organisation (FAO) commissioned a study in Africa involving 1.9 million hectares of organic land and 2 million small-scale farmers. It found that good organic farming practices doubled yields compared with those from traditional subsistence farming.[93]

A long-term systems comparison conducted by FiBL, the Swiss Research Institute of Organic Agriculture, in cooperation with local partners has shown that organic farming techniques increase the income of small-scale farmers. In Kenya, where 60 small-scale farmers were involved in the project, farmers have reduced production costs and increased prices obtained at market. After five years, organic cultivation is more profitable than conventional intensive agriculture. After six years, the returns from organic farming are actually 53% higher. Parallel long-term studies by FiBL of cotton production in India and coffee in Bolivia also show higher returns with organic methods.[94]

Diagram 2 | Comparison of incomes from different cultivation systems in Chuka

Cumulative gross profit per hectare in USD

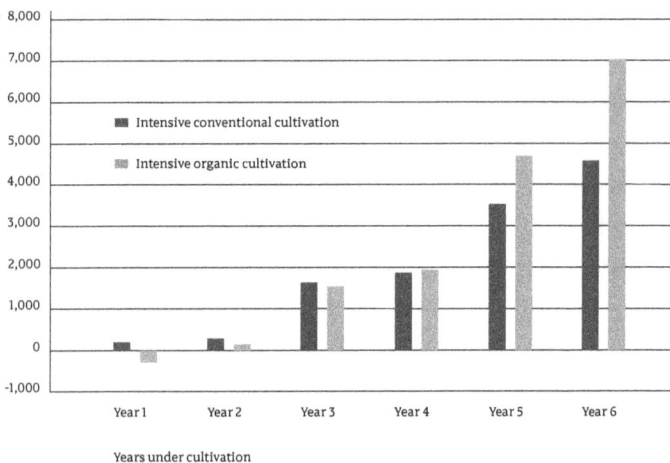

Years under cultivation

In 1990, the land under organic cultivation in the world was in the low one-thousandths. By 2010, this figure had increased to 2%. The global market for organic food and drinks increased in value between 1999 and 2009 from US$ 15 billion to just under US$ 55 billion,[95] and by 2014 it had increased further to US$ 80 billion.[96]

Protect and regenerate agricultural soils

The loss of agricultural land must be halted. Good land must be retained for farming and not built on. This requires strong political will.

In order to curb soil degradation, we must take active steps, e.g. plant new tree belts and hedges to protect fields from water and wind erosion. In particular, however, we need to stop the practices that are damaging the soil in the first place: over-fertilisation, overexploitation, soil compaction from the use of heavy machinery and unnecessary ploughing or plough-ing too deep.

The plough is one of the stupidest things ever invented by humans. It not only increases the likelihood of soil erosion but the action of turning over the soil destroys its natural struc-ture and damages its biotic community. The worms, insects and microorganisms living in the deeper layers are violently forced to the surface. Conversely, the fauna adapted to living on the surface is pushed down into the soil and perishes. An-other serious consequence of ploughing is that it releases car-bon dioxide sequestered in the soil (see also Section "Agricul-ture and climate protection") below.

Traditionally, the purpose of the plough was to turn over the top layer of the soil and bury the weeds. This protected the next seed crop. However, weeds can be controlled in other ways and without the use of herbicides. There are simple machines that loosely break up the soil and cover the plant material left over from the harvest with a little soil. This forms a thin compost layer that fertilises the soil and at the same time suppresses weeds. The seed is sown with a small no-till machine that only produces narrow furrows. In addition, cereal crops can be alternated with beans; they produce nitrogen and so add nitrogen naturally to the soil. The crop can be also used as fodder for livestock and the manure from the livestock is then available as a soil fertiliser.

Halting and reversing land degradation is one of the Sustainable Development Goals agreed at the UN Conference on Sustainable Development in Rio de Janeiro (Rio+20) to be achieved by 2030 (see also Chapter 7 "IAASTD Report and its consequences"). Whilst this is welcome, it is not enough. To guarantee food supplies for future generations, we need to include the soils that are already leached or will be 2030. These soils must be regenerated so that they too can be used for sustainable production. In addition, regeneration methods must be less greedy in terms of energy inputs and be affordable for farmers in developing countries. Compost can play an important role here.

Stop using pesticides

Healthy plants thriving in healthy soils are more resistant to pests and disease. They can compete more effectively with weeds. Biological methods of plant protection still have much to offer, but to exploit them fully we need additional investment in research and teaching. Pesticides should only be used if farmers are unable to manage pests with natural methods. In that case, biological products should be made available to farmers, e.g. soft soaps, neem powder or pyrethrum.

Integrated Pest Management (IPM) is the term used for systems that effectively coordinate the use of all available processes, including pesticides in an emergency. The aim is to keep the level of damaging organisms to below the Economic Injury Level (EIL) whilst focussing wherever possible on the use of natural control mechanisms. As part of a regional programme run by the FAO in West Africa, 30,000 farmers were trained in IPM; pesticide use declined on average by 75%, yields increased by 23% and earnings rose by 41%.[97]

Save water
Improved irrigation techniques, e.g. drip irrigation and underground piped water systems, also have the potential to deliver significant improvements. They can increase yields by up to 100% whilst reducing water consumption by 40–80%.[98]

Small-scale ecological farming can also help to reduce water consumption. The Green Economy Report (see section at the end of this chapter) published in 2011 by UNEP, the United Nations Environment Programme, concluded that sustainable farming methods could supply enough food to meet the needs of the global population in 2050 and yet use less water than now.[99]

In addition, it would help if we stopped growing water-intensive crops, such as maize and cotton, in areas that are too dry. We should be retaining or replanting forests that store water. Reductions in water consumption can also protect soils. Excessive irrigation causes soil run-off and so contributes to soil erosion. In contrast, methods that protect the soil, including the regeneration of degraded soils, can reduce water consumption. This is because living soils rich in humus are also good for water storage.

Diagram 3 | Predicted changes in agricultural production by 2080 as a result of climate change, taking into account possible increases in fertility from increases in CO_2. [Map based on Cline, 2007]

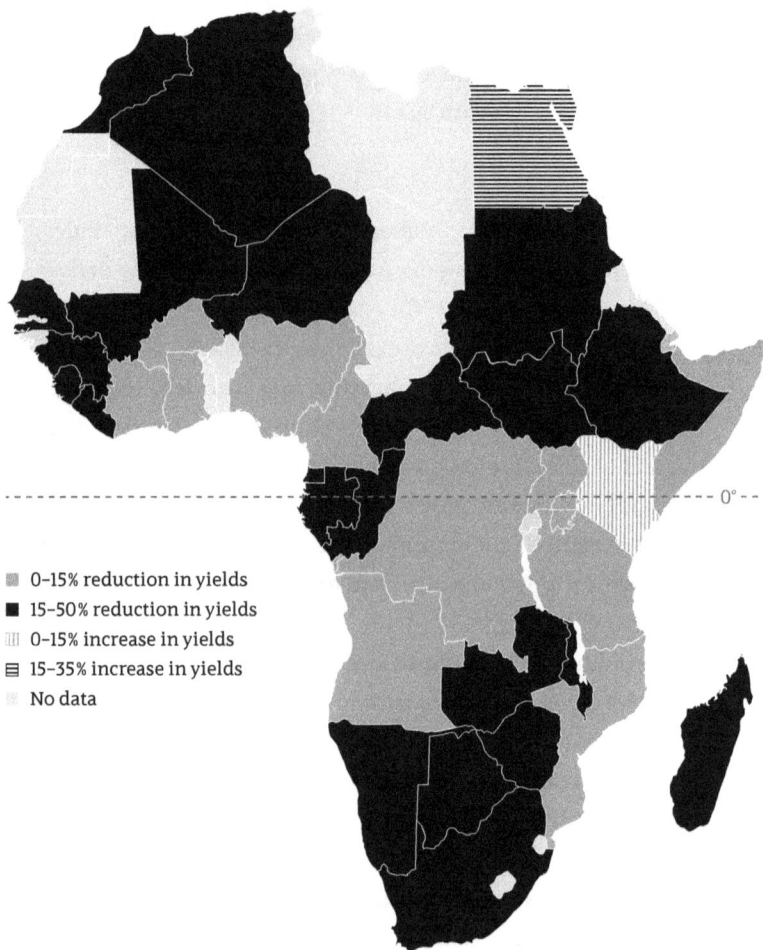

- 0–15% reduction in yields
- 15–50% reduction in yields
- 0–15% increase in yields
- 15–35% increase in yields
- No data

0°

Encourage biodiversity

Seed diversity can be retained and encouraged if small-scale farmers are able to use their own seed. Ecological agriculture also serves to maintain and encourage the biodiversity of wild flora and fauna. Long-term trials by FiBL, the Swiss Research Institute of Organic Agriculture, have shown that organic arable fields and grassland are significantly richer in soil life than conventional farmland. The number of earthworms in organic soils is 50–80% higher. Other soil-based animals, such as ground beetles, spiders and rove beetles, are twice as common. The number of bacteria, fungi, protozoa and algae can be as much as 85% higher.[100]

Agriculture and climate protection

If we are to limit global warming, it is not enough just to abandon fossil fuels. Even if we stopped their emissions immediately, temperatures would continue to rise because climate systems take time to respond, also if the atmospheric CO_2 content remain unchanged. There is, therefore, a risk the Earth will emit huge quantities of greenhouse gases as the permafrost thaws. So we also need to remove atmospheric CO_2, and agriculture can play a crucial role in this process.

Plants absorb CO_2 from the air through the process of photosynthesis. Some of the carbon absorbed in this way reaches the soil through roots, root exudates and dead plant material. Organisms living in the soil decompose the plant material and form humus. The result is extremely stable organic substances that can survive for decades in the soil. The carbon now floating in the atmosphere originally came from the soil. Humus stores large quantities of carbon from the atmosphere, and it is estimated that the top 30 cm of the soil contains as much carbon as there is in the atmosphere.[101]

In the past, it was considerably more. Converting forests and grassland into arable land releases vast quantities of carbon. Scientists estimate that soils have emitted 136 billion tonnes of carbon into the atmosphere since the start of industrialisation.[102]

If the ecological balance of agriculture were restored, it would return at least some of the carbon to the soil.

The following are important for carbon storage:
- No pesticides. They kill the soil organisms that are crucial to carbon storage.
- No mineral fertilisers. They also damage soil life. A study in the United States showed that the carbon content of soil increased by 2.47 tonnes per hectare when arable fields were fertilised solely with compost and a system of crop rotation was adopted. In contrast, fields treated with artificial fertilisers and without crop rotation lost 0.37 tonnes of carbon per year.[103]
- Minimal soil tillage. Ploughing releases carbon.
- Complete plant cover using intercropping techniques. Carbon also leaks from soils left fallow.
- Crop diversity and rotation. This encourages a diverse soil life.
- Appropriate grazing of permanent grassland.

The Northeast Organic Farming Association in Massachusetts (USA) has estimated that the consistent use of methods designed to maximise carbon storage on all arable land and pasture in the world would remove 23.7 billion tonnes of carbon annually from the atmosphere.[104]

Of course, the soil cannot store an infinite amount of carbon and eventually it will be full. However, it would help enormously if we could return to the soil most of the carbon released into the atmosphere during the last 250 years as a result of changes in land use.

In pre-industrial times, the CO_2 content in the atmosphere was 280 ppm (parts per million); it is now 400 ppm. One ppm of CO_2 represents 2,125 billion tonnes of carbon.[105] If we returned 10,625 billion tonnes into the soil, this would reduce the amount in the atmosphere by 50 ppm CO_2.

The realisation that we need to increase the carbon content of soil is gaining ground in international climate politics. The French government has launched an international research project "4 pour mille", which aims to increase the carbon content of soils globally by 4 per 1000. If this amount of CO_2 were stored annually, it would offset current man-made emissions and the atmospheric content would cease to rise.[106]

The basic techniques of organic agriculture include several methods that increase the carbon content of soil. An analysis in 2012 of 74 studies published in a wide range of countries showed that the carbon content of organic soils was on average 3.5 tonnes per hectare higher than soils managed conventionally.[107]

There is a further reason why organic agriculture is climate-friendly. It requires huge quantities of oil to produce pesticides and mineral fertilisers. Greenhouse gas emissions from ecological farming are much lower than from conventional agriculture. This is because the former manages largely without agrochemicals. Greenhouse gas emissions generated by the production of one kilogram of organic wheat bread are 23–25% lower than those from the production of one kilogram of conventionally produced bread. Organic bread has a better CO_2 balance because it does not use nitrogen fertilisers.[108]

Multifunctionality

Multifunctionality is a central tenet of a refocussed agricultural policy. In this case, farmers not only produce food but also provide a public benefit by protecting the climate, controlling water pollution, maintaining biodiversity and managing the landscape. In Switzerland, farmers are paid a total of 1.4 billion Swiss francs from the public purse each year in return for providing services for the common good.[109]

Agriculture in developing countries is no less multi-functional and so farmers in the global South should also be paid a financial reward for providing a public benefit. For example, the money could come from the funding streams available under international biodiversity or climate policies. In this case we would need to improve the techniques for measuring carbon in the soil so that we could quantify the services provided by ecological agriculture that benefit the climate and pay a fair reward.

Fight waste

The FAO has indicated that losses in the supply chain from field to fork could be reduced by 50% within a reasonable timescale.[110]

In order to reduce food losses in developing countries, we need to improve certain parts of the food chain from grower to consumer, e.g. better production planning based on market conditions; more efficient use of resources in production and processing; better techniques for the storage, packaging and preservation of food; and better transport links. In part, this requires improvements to existing technologies or the development of new ones. Public funds must be used to encourage local innovation, such as zero-energy cooling systems.

Consumers in industrial countries need a better understanding of the value of foodstuffs, and by this we mean the true price of food. We waste things that are cheap. Investment in measures to reduce production, storage and transport losses is only worthwhile if the cost of that investment is less than the value of the foods no longer left to rot. Consumers in industrial countries would probably waste less if it hurt their wallet.

Global fair trade

In order to increase production, we need trading conditions that are reasonably fair. Liberalising agricultural trade can only benefit developing countries if those countries are treated as equal partners in the discussions. This is not currently the case.

If we are to transform agriculture, we need to include trading practices. Trade rules must be formulated so that small-scale farmers receive a fair share. OECD countries must re-think their policies on subsidies and trading. Export subsidies expose farmers in developing countries to unfair competition, undermine food security and stifle production. These subsidies must be changed into payments for services to the ecosystem.

In addition, we need to pay fair prices for exported produce and pay agricultural workers a decent wage. The daily amount paid to coffee pickers in Kenya would currently buy you just one litre of milk even though coffee prices on the world market have doubled in the last five years!

The fair trade system is one approach: according to the umbrella body Fairtrade Labelling Organizations International, more than 1.5 million farmers currently benefit from fair trade.[111]

Food sovereignty

The concept of a liberalised agriculture market has to be set against the concept of food sovereignty. Each country should have the right to define its own agriculture and food policies. Developing countries must be allowed to pay subsidies to their farmers and impose import tariffs until domestic agriculture is competitive. Economic cooperation with regions at risk from hunger should be negotiated on an individual basis as conditions vary from country to country.

Food will always be imported and exported; trade serves to balance demand and supply and makes available produce that cannot be grown locally, e.g. tropical fruit in temperate latitudes. This not only makes ecological sense but is also economically and socially prudent.

Nevertheless, each country should seek to produce as much food as possible locally and sustainably. This will not only reduce its dependence on imports but also make it less vulnerable to the effects of adverse conditions, such as bad weather, disease or pest infestations.

Refocus research and technology

This change in direction demands a fundamental realignment of agricultural research and development. The paradigm for current research operations remains profit maximisation. In addition, research is geared to the needs of industrial agriculture and the profitable cash-crops produced by large-scale farmers. It focusses mainly on global markets. Current research has next to nothing to offer small-scale farmers. Moreover, agroecology rarely finds a voice in research. For example, in Switzerland the agricultural research institutes of Agroscope, the centre of excellence of the Swiss Confederation for agricultural research, receives 170 million Swiss francs each year whereas the Research Institute of Organic Agriculture FiBL has to make do with just 4.5 million.

This must change. We need broad-based, multidisciplinary agricultural research focussing on sustainability and new issues:

- How do plants interact with each other and with soil organisms? How do plants replace water and nutrients? How do plants support each other in order to resist pests and disease pathogens?
- How does soil life function? How can we improve soil fertility? How can we increase the carbon content of soils?
- How can we exploit the potential offered by ancient varieties in order to breed and produce varieties that are resistant to both heat and drought?
- How can we increase the range of biological processes for plant protection and so provide an effective process for each pest?
- How can we improve irrigation techniques and so drastically reduce water consumption?
- What is the most effective way for agriculture to fight poverty, inequality, gender discrimination and help improve human health?

For this to happen, we need thousands of institutions like FiBL. There is no single system that is right for modern agriculture. Rather the world needs many different systems, and to do justice to this wide variety, we need local approaches. Research must be shifted from the laboratory to the field, and there should be better integration between local farmers and regional research networks.

Research must increasingly return to the public sector so that funding can be allocated on a non-profit basis. In addition, research must include stakeholders from multiple sectors: agriculture, various scientific disciplines, industry, environment and health. Politicians and civil society should have an increasing role and a greater say in decisions on the choice of research objectives and projects. Only then can we achieve the level of innovation required by the global food system.

Generate and exchange knowledge

Knowledge is the only resource that grows when shared with others—and it must grow. The knowledge and new methods coming out of agricultural research must also reach local people. Farmers need a good education and must be able to participate in an intensive exchange of knowledge, including new IT and communications technology.

This exchange of knowledge must be a two-way process. It is essential that traditional local knowledge of relevance to new developments is able to feed into agriculture research. New partnerships between farmers, researchers and agricultural engineers can ensure a benefit for all.

Genetic engineering is not the answer

Promises that genetically modified wheat varieties can withstand drought and thrive on extremely poor soils are nothing more than a temporary utopia. What is more, even if there were such varieties, they would still be unaffordable for small-scale farmers. Genetic engineering also entrenches unsustainable systems of cultivation because they rely unduly on artificial fertilisers, pesticides and monocultures.

As part of the preparatory work for the IAASTD Report published in 2008 (see Chapter 7 "IAASTD Report and its consequences"), scientists reviewed a large number of studies on the use of genetic engineering in agriculture. In essence, the review found that genetic engineering currently offer almost nothing to those people who are starving.

Similarly, the purpose of the current genetically modified varieties is not to improve the food situation. First and foremost, they have been developed for herbicide resistance and so allow farmers to spray total herbicides without damaging crops. The genetically modified seed varieties available from all the major pesticide companies—mainly maize, oilseed rape, cotton and soya—contain genes that make them resistant to the herbicide produced by the company selling that variety.

This means that we are breeding problem weeds. In the United States, the use of plants with a gene that makes them resistant to the total herbicide glyphosate has resulted in the spread of weeds that are resistant to glyphosate. In 2012, this was affecting an area of 25 million hectares.[112]

The other focus has been the introduction of genes that codify the production of the microbe *Bacillus thuringiensis* (Bt); this microbe contains a protein that poisons harmful pests. Bt has been successfully used as a natural insecticide for decades as it is not harmful to vertebrates and is also biodegradable. The risk now is that the protein is becoming less effective as pests are increasingly developing a resistance to it—mainly as a result of the widespread cultivation of Bt maize and Bt cotton.

A case in point is the western corn rootworm (*Diabrotica virgifera virgifera*), a bug that is the main cause of damage to maize in the United States and Canada. It is known colloquially as the "billion dollar pest". In 2003, the US seed and herbicide manufacturer Monsanto brought out a Bt maize that killed the corn rootworm. Even though this solved the farmers' immediate problem, their relief was short-lived. The first rootworms resistant to the Bt in the Monsanto genetically modified maize appeared in 2011. In the interim, other seed firms had developed genetically modified varieties containing other Bt genes. However, they too only provided a brief respite for farmers. The corn rootworms that had developed a resistance to the Monsanto BT maize also developed a resistance to these other products. As a result the "billion dollar pest" is back in the maize fields of North America.[113] To sum up: Bt, an organic product used successfully without causing damage, was incorporated into a new product. As a result, the insects were under permanent pressure and thus developed a resistance. In the process, organic farmers have lost an important pest control agent.

Similarly, golden rice promised a permanent benefit. This is a genetically modified variety of rice that produces vitamin A. Nobody is disputing the fact that vitamin A deficiencies are a serious health issue. The World Health Organisation (WHO) has estimated that more than 250 million children suffer from the deficiency worldwide. Between 250,000 and 500,000 go blind and some 50% of these die within one year of losing their sight.[114] However, golden rice has not fulfilled its promise. Despite research lasting 20 years that had broad support and involved a huge financial investment, the world still has no rice variety ready for cultivation that can reliably produce enough vitamin A now and for several generations to come that is capable of eliminating the deficiency in humans.[115]

In principle, any attempt to remedy a vitamin A deficiency with a genetically modified rice variety is bound to fail, not least because it adopts a reductionist approach. The use of patents to solve hunger and vitamin deficiencies will simply not work. People who lack vitamin A are not only short of vitamins. They lack food and are unable to feed themselves properly. The issue is linked to poverty and a range of other interrelated factors. We need holistic solutions that provide those affected with enough food and a balanced diet.

Many foods are rich in vitamin A, but often they rot in storage areas or under trees close to where the hungry are living. One possible alternative is the orange-fleshed sweet potato grown as part of a crop rotation system. It has been developed by four scientists: Dr Maria Andrade from the Cape Verde Islands, Dr Howarth Bouis and Dr Jan Low from the United States and Dr Robert Mwanga from Uganda. They are using biofortification in order to tackle hunger and malnourishment. Biofortification is a process of selective breeding that increases the nutrient value of food crops by adding vital vitamins and minerals. In 2016, the scientists were awarded the World Food Prize for their work.[116]

The pattern is always the same: A problem arises. The agri-business sector offers a patented solution using a genetically modified seed. This works for a while, sometimes, but the old problem soon returns—and we have an extra one as well.

We must give up on such quick fixes; they only treat the symptoms. We need to tackle the root cause of the problem. We must treat agriculture as a system and all sectors must look at the issue. We must firmly reject the patenting of plants. After all, it is farmers we have to thank for the huge variety of plants and livestock breeds. This wealth must remain with the people.

Green Economy Report

In the run-up to the Earth Summit (Rio+20), UNEP, the United Nations Environment Programme, published its Green Economy Report. It called for a permanent investment of 2% of global GDP to bring about a change to a low-carbon, resource-efficient global economy. Of this, a total of 198 billion US dollars, or 0.16% of global GDP, should feed into agriculture.[117]

The investment was needed to regenerate degraded soils, promote diversified farming combining crops and livestock, fight erosion, improve irrigation systems, introduce biological pest control, improve the access by small-scale farmers to markets, and reduce the losses between harvest and consumption.

The authors of the chapter on agriculture completed a modelling exercise for the period until 2050. It compared a green scenario, i.e. one that assumed that agriculture followed the above principles with a brown scenario, i.e. one that assumed we continued unchanged with current agricultural practices. The superiority of the green scenario was impressive. With the green scenario, the world could increase food availability from the current 2,800 kilocalories per day per head to a satisfactory 3,300 kilocalories. The green scenario would create 47 million more jobs in rural areas than the brown scenario and so help to reduce poverty. The green scenario would use less water than today, whereas water consumption would increase by 40% with the brown scenario. With the green scenario we would only need to clear 7 million hectares of forest rather than 15 million hectares.[118] Finally, with the green scenario agriculture would be a key player in climate protection by 2050 rather than an emitter of greenhouse gases.

A global sustainable food system that conserves resources and provides healthy food is not solely the responsibility of farmers, politicians and industry. Consumers, including those in rich industrial countries, have a responsibility to change their lifestyles.

Curb our appetite for meat

In Chapter 1, I mentioned the high levels of meat consumption and the associated problems. If global population increases by a further three to four billion people and if improvements in living standards translate into higher meat consumption to the current levels in rich countries, the world will be unable to produce enough meat. We do not have enough farmland or water to produce that amount of food and animal feed.

A diet rich in meat is also associated with high greenhouse emissions. WWF Switzerland commissioned ESU Services, a specialist in lifecycle assessments, to calculate the balance of greenhouse gases for different diets in Switzerland. Greenhouse gas emissions per head of population, including the "grey" emissions in imported goods, are currently 12.8 tonnes of CO_2 equivalent (CO_2e); of this more than 1.8 tonnes are attributable to food.[119] For vegans it is only 1.1 tonnes and for vegetarians 1.4 tonnes. A moderate meat eater—who consumes about 300 g per week—causes 1.5 tonnes of emissions and for a big meat eater—who consumes 2 kg per week (double the average consumption)—the figure is 2.3 tonnes.[120]

Kg CO₂e per year and per person

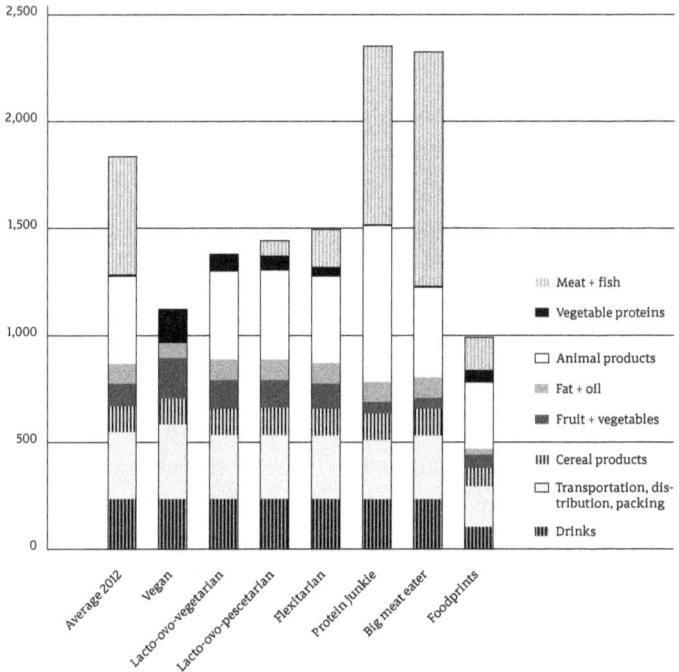

Diagram 4 | Greenhouse gas balance by dietary type and by food groups (kg CO_2e per year and per person)

Legend:
- Meat + fish
- Vegetable proteins
- Animal products
- Fat + oil
- Fruit + vegetables
- Cereal products
- Transportation, distribution, packing
- Drinks

Categories: Average 2012, Vegan, Lacto-ovo-vegetarian, Lacto-ovo-pescetarian, Flexitarian, Protein junkie, Big meat eater, Foodprints

If we reduced individual meat consumption each year by one kilogram, diet-related greenhouse emissions would decline by 10 kg CO_2 equivalents. Reductions in meat consumption would also allow us to keep livestock in more appropriate conditions. Conditions would vary depending upon the species but would include more space for animals outdoors and indoors. It would also be good for our digestions. A healthy diet contains a variety of foods, particularly plant-based foods and a weekly meat consumption of 300 g to 600 g of meat, or 16.5 kg to 3 kg per year. One can also note that grassfed beef, for example, is rich in

Environmental impact scores 2013 per year and person

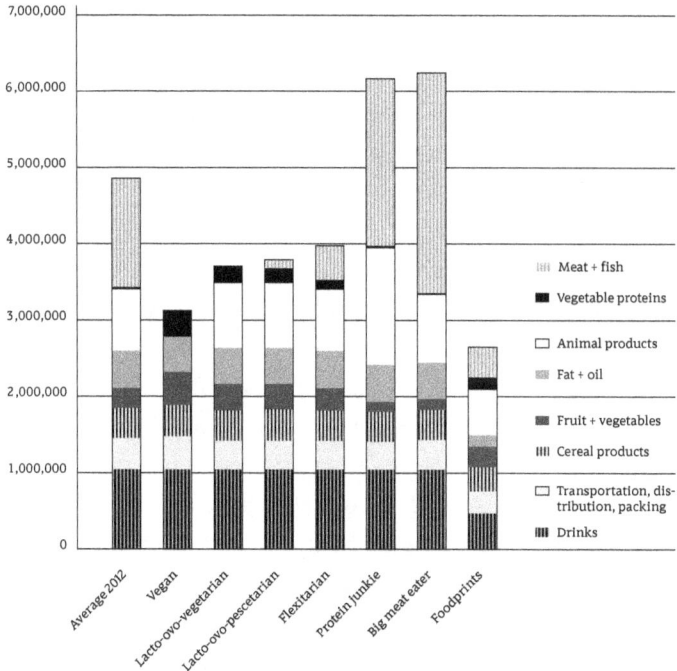

Omega 3 and low in Omega 6, the healthy balance if one wants to consume red meat.

The Chinese government has set a target of reducing meat consumption by half. In the last 40 years, meat consumption has increased sixfold in China and consumption per capita now equals that of Germany. Using public information campaigns, the government will seek to reduce annual meat consumption in China to just 27 kg per person.[121] This figure is included in guidelines published by the Chinese Ministry of Health, which plans to update them every ten years. In introducing this action, it has cited climate protection and the health benefits of a low-meat diet.

In India, such a campaign is unnecessary. Despite similar growth figures to China, meat consumption in India has stagnated since 1969 at 4 kg per person per year. It would appear that an increase in meat consumption with rising incomes is not necessarily a law of nature. Dietary habits are also the result of culture and culture can be changed.[122]

Rethink mobility patterns

Our mobility patterns are far from being sustainable. Plants grown for fuel reduce the land available for food and this impacts on global nutrition. The production of biofuels—ethanol from sugar cane or maize and methyl ester from soya and oilseed rape—tripled between 2000 and 2008.[123] One-third of maize production in the United States ends up in the fuel tank.

Climate protection has been cited as justification for the development of biofuels with the argument that the CO_2 balance of renewables is better than that of fossil fuels. The effect, however, is minimal whereas the land take is huge. Some 8 million hectares of agricultural land is needed in order to replace 1% of global diesel and petrol consumption with biofuels—an area approximately twice the size of the Netherlands.

Our addiction to mobility is depriving farmers of land for food production. In addition, analyses in Switzerland have shown that the eco-balance of all energy crops is far worse than it is for petrol and diesel. Energy crops require intensive methods of cultivation and so have a greater impact on environmental pollution. The only fuels that would actually benefit the environment are those made from waste products, e.g. from used cooking oil, timber waste or compostable waste.[124]

Remain on the ground

The emissions from air travel are particularly high and growing rapidly. A flight from Zurich to New York and back emits 2.24 tonnes of CO_2. A flight to Rio de Janeiro and back emits 3.33 tonnes and a short-haul flight to London and back 0.58 tonnes of CO_2.[125]

In the medium term, we can switch to electric vehicles, but it is hard to imagine air travel without CO_2 emissions. Jet setting is a thing of the past. To be ahead of the crowd, remain on the ground. With new technology, it is easy to hold virtual meetings.

7. IAASTD Report and its consequences

In 2008, a panel of agricultural professionals from around the world published a road map for sustainable agriculture: the report—the International Assessment of Agricultural Science & Technology for Development (IAASTD) Report.[126] It put forward strategies and measures that would transform agriculture and make it fit for future challenges, e.g. rises in global population, increases in demand and climate change. It was prompted by reports from the FAO and the World Bank.

IASSTD and its messages did not please everyone. Syngenta, one of the largest agribusinesses in the world with its head office in Basle, and the international agricultural association CropLife were initially involved drafting the assessment. However, they decided to opt out in early 2008 when they saw a draft of the report. Ecological agriculture is not a good customer for agribusinesses, who earn their money from selling high-yielding seed varieties, fertilisers and pesticides.

A coalition of major agri-giants in the United States, Canada and Australia and their friends in Brazil and Argentina are still intent on expanding industrial agriculture. They meet in Davos at the World Economic Forum and at G8 and G20 summits. It is these multinational agrochemical and biotech companies plus other major players such as the Gates and Rockefeller Foundations who are now the major investors in a type of agriculture that is certainly not sustainable. They have largely taken over the role of governments.

Despite that, the agricultural industry has been put on the back foot. In many countries, IAASTD is taken seriously, including by government leaders. For example, the African Union has launched an initiative to introduce organic agriculture and this initiative is being implemented in eight different countries.

Initially, the FAO reacted cautiously to the report. However, slowly but surely its attitude has thawed. This was evident from articles on the FAO's website posted to coincide with the launch of the Year of Family Farming in 2014. The FAO is now calling for more sustainable agriculture, and ecological intensification, and in 2014, the organisation even held a symposium on agroecology, which was followed up with 5 regional agroecology workshops around the globe in 2015 and 2016.[127]

The Agricultural Technology for Development Report presented to the UN General Assembly in 2015 also took on board the main messages and demands of IAASTD. It analysed the development of agrotechnology and the ecological and social problems of the current food system. It came to similar conclusions and has suggested a radical shift towards sustainable systems. It called for "ecological intensification" as an alternative to the paradigm of the Green Revolution. It recommended a greater emphasis on ecological agriculture and the continued development of associated technologies. Climate-neutral agriculture should be a primary objective.[128]

Similarly, the World Bank and the International Food Policy Research Institute (IFPRI) are amongst those calling for more sustainable agriculture. We are seeing an increasing reference to small-scale farmers and the crucial role played by women; in some cases, even past mistakes are being acknowledged.

UNCTAD, the United Nations Conference on Trade and Development, supported the IAASTD Report from the outset. In its most recent Trade and Environment Report in 2013, it reiterated the main messages of IAASTD, i.e. a move away from industrial agricultural production, diversity not monocultures, and agroecological methods instead of mineral fertilisers and pesticides. In particular, it called for more support for small-scale farmers. UNCTAD concluded that the transformation of agriculture was one of the greatest challenges of the century.

Sustainable Development Goals

In 2012, the United Nations Conference on Sustainable Development in Rio de Janeiro (Rio+20) agreed to develop sustainable development goals for the period after 2015. Agenda 2030 with its 17 Sustainable Development Goals (SDGs) was negotiated over a three-year period and accepted by all UN member states in September 2015.[129] The agenda is binding on all countries and, unlike the Millennium Development Goals, is designed to pave the way for a better future in both developed and developing countries. Global sustainable development must be more than just a green-tinged business as usual.

The SDGs seek to eliminate poverty and ensure that everyone has access to clean water, reliable and sustainably produced energy, healthcare and education. They call for equality between women and men, a reduction in inequalities both between and within countries and full employment through sustainable economic growth. Other goals include the protection of oceans, the maintenance and restoration of terrestrial ecosystems, and measures to limit and adapt to climate change. Stronger global partnerships will be needed in order to achieve these goals.

SDG 2 relates directly to agriculture: "End hunger, achieve food security and improved nutrition, and promote sustainable agriculture." By 2030, everyone should have year-round access to sufficient food. The aim is to double the incomes of small-scale farmers and improve the lives of women. Sustainable systems should guarantee food production, contribute to the preservation of ecosystems, increase our ability to adapt to climate change and improve soil quality. As early as 2020, the genetic diversity of seed, crops, livestock and related wild species should be guaranteed.

Agricultural production in developing countries should be increased by investing in rural infrastructure, agricultural research, advisory services and greater international cooperation. Trade distortions on global agricultural markets should be corrected, including the elimination of all types of agricultural export subsidies.

The Committee on World Food Security (CFS) has been tasked to support individual nations in switching to sustainable agriculture. To do this, it will draw on the IAASTD recommendations and involve not only representatives from governments, business and science but also representatives from agriculture and civil society.

My own two organisations, Biovision and the Millennium Institute, closely monitored the negotiations leading up to the SDG agreement. As part of our project Changing Course in Global Agriculture, we submitted detailed evidence and draft proposals based on our years of experience to government negotiators. We reiterated our position at a variety of events and in bilateral discussions. In particular, we were able to make a significant contribution to SDG 2 "Zero hunger", partly because Biovision was the only Swiss organisation with general consultative status of ECOSOC, the UN Economic and Social Council.

There is only one world. We should all be singing from the same hymn sheet. Unfortunately, this is still not the case. The North must stop defending its edge over developing countries. On the other hand, developing countries must stop insisting on the same growth model as that previously adopted by industrial countries. We can no longer pursue a model where everyone is out to get what they can from others. No one needs to "feed" the world. Agriculture and food systems need to be re-localised, countries need to assert their food sovereignty, and at the same time there will also be international trade to cover for disasters that may and will occur occasionally.

The Sustainable Development Goals are our last real chance to do something right for future generations. The best thing about them is that they are universal. Switzerland must keep to them as must Botswana.

There are grounds for hope, the greatest of which is the number of farmers throughout the world who are implementing sustainable forms of food production at a local level.

My father always said that a pessimist will never achieve great things. A pessimist sees the difficulty in every opportunity; an optimist sees the opportunity in every difficulty. If we lose our optimism, we have nothing left. I will continue to fight for this until my last breath.

MY VISION IN PRACTICE

The holy mountain is turning green again

MARIMANTI, KENYA

"Life was good here in the past," explains the 82-year old Neftali Kian'a Miru from Marimanti, a village in the hot and arid Tharaka Plain. "We had enough to eat and people respected nature." But in the meantime, a lot more people live in this hot and dry region near the equator and they all need land and wood. The forests have shrunk, and even areas on Ntugi Hill, a holy mountain and place of their ancestors, have been cleared. There has been much less rain in recent years and droughts have increased.

More and more arable farmers have switched to modern hybrid varieties that produce a higher yield. But the seeds are expensive and the farmers cannot produce these hybrid seeds themselves. These new varieties cannot cope with the dry climate in Tharaka and the crops soon wither. In 2009, many families had to rely on food aid and earned nothing from their work in the fields.

Neftali's widowed daughter Sabella had to sell all her cattle in order to feed her three children. Sabella realised that things had to change. She joined a group of farmers who are taking part in an initiative run by the Institute for Culture and Ecology (ICE), a Kenyan NGO and one of Biovision's local partners. ICE is committed to protecting the environment, maintaining traditional cultures and working to improve the lives of rural communities. In particular, it encourages farmers to use a combination of traditional knowledge and modern, organic methods of cultivation. ICE also provides farmers with forgotten local agricultural crops.

ICE advisors train farmers from Marimanti in methods of organic cultivation and show them how erosion can be slowed and how the soil can be improved with compost. And they provide them with seeds and agricultural crops that are resistant to droughts.

Today, Sabella is cultivating five different types of finger millet and eleven species of sorghum. She grows five types of mung beans, eight types of cowpeas and three pea varieties. "Demand for my produce is high and the sale of seeds is also going very well," she says contentedly. Last year, she earned 50,000 Kenyan shillings (about 400 euros) just from seed sales, which was just enough to finance her son's education.

Her farmer group has also started to plant trees. The holy Ntugi Hill is already turning green again.[130]

P. 68 | Ikwa, a waterfall on Kathita River in Tharaka (Kenya), is a place of their ancestors for the people living there and thus a holy place. Such holy places like Ikwa and the Ntugi Hill are threatened by the increasing demand for firewood and wooden building material. By educating people and with reforesting activities, Sabella Kian'a and her farmer group are engaged in maintaining these natural holy places.

P. 69 top | Farmland can be maintained with compost and improved with ecological means. In many projects of Biovision, practical knowledge about composting is disseminated, including in Marimanti (Tharaka, Kenya).

P. 69 bottom | Fertile soil is fundamental for the production of food. Worldwide, and especially in Africa, such soils are being lost. The photo shows erosion near Marimanti.

Push-Pull keeps pests and weeds in check

Maize is a staple food in East Africa and is grown on most small family farms. However, pests such as the stemborer moth and weeds such as *Striga* (witchweed) are widespread. They can cause massive damage to harvests and in some cases wipe them out completely. Most families are unable to afford chemical pesticides and fertilizers; they also have a detrimental effect on biodiversity.

Push-Pull is a biological solution to the problem and was developed by Professor Zeyaur Khan from the International Centre of Insect Physiology and Ecology (*icipe*) in Nairobi. It is based on a mixed-cropping system whereby desmodium, a member of the flowering family *Fabaceae* is grown between maize plants. The smell from the desmodium repels the stemborer moths (the "push" aspect). A further benefit is that desmodium increases the nitrogen content of the soil. As a legume, it has a symbiotic relationship with the root bacteria and so fixes nitrogen. Last but not least, desmodium neutralises weeds in the genus *Striga*.

Napier grass is planted around the edge of the field and attracts the stemborer moth (the "pull" aspect). When the moth larvae end up on the sticky leaves they perish. This method of natural weed and pest control, which was developed by *icipe* in Nairobi, can increase maize yields by up to 300%. In addition, desmodium and napier grass provide nutritious fodder for the cattle; this in turn increases milk production.

At the start of this century, the Push-Pull method was almost unknown. It is now used on more than 120,000 farms in East Africa. It was also expressly cited as an innovative approach for sustainable agriculture in the Agricultural Technology for Development Report submitted to the UN General Assembly in October 2015.[131]

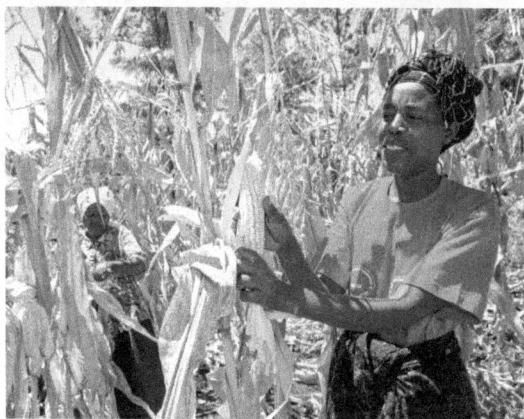

Left | Napier grass and desmodium, the basis of the Push-Pull method, provide top-quality cattle feed, and allow farmers to significantly increase milk yields.

Top right | The research fields at the *icipe* research institute in Mbita Point on Lake Victoria (Kenya) are used for scientific trials of various species of desmodium to see which are suitable as "push" plants.

Bottom right | The Push-Pull method can increase maize yields on a sustainable basis by up to 300%.

Test fields comparing Push-Pull and conventional methods. The field trial at the *icipe* research institute in Mbita Point demonstrates the clear difference between a Push-Pull field (left) and a conventional field (right).

The desmodium planted between the maize plants also controls the *Striga* weed that significantly reduces crop yields. As a legume, desmodium increases soil fertility, improves moisture retention and protects fields from erosion.

Target: 100% organic

Bhutan is currently listed 136 out of 175 in the rankings for average per capita income, life expectancy and educational attainment.[132] Two-thirds of the population work in agriculture. Even though only 3% of the country's landmass—the fertile valleys—is suitable for arable farming, Bhutan is largely self-sufficient with the exception of rice. Eighty per cent of the country is forested and should remain so—the laws on nature conservation demand that.

In 2008, the Bhutanese government signed the IAASTD Report. In fact, it went even further and started to introduce the required changes to national agriculture policies. In 2012, its Minister of Agriculture Pema Gyamtsho—himself a farmer—announced the aim of switching all farming to organic production. Initially, government intervention has focussed on providing information, advice and training. It is also hoped that the export of organic produce will generate new sources of income for the rural population and so put a halt to the rural exodus.

"It is a widespread myth that we actually had a choice when opting to switch to organic farming," explained Jigmi Thinley, Bhutan's Prime Minister at Rio+20, the United Nations Conference on Sustainable Development in 2012. "In terms of food security, we had no choice; it was an issue of survival."[133]

Open field days for organic farming

SACDEP, KENYA

In Kenya, some 70% of the population earn their living from agriculture and yet almost 30% of the population remain malnourished. Most smallholders farm only 2–3 hectares of barren land.

In 1993, the Kenyan agronomist Ngugi Mutura set up an NGO called the Sustainable Agriculture Community Development Programme (SACDEP). Its priorities are organic farming, crop cultivation adapted to local conditions, water management, small animal husbandry, renewable energies and a system of microloans. SACDEP has trained groups of 30 to 40 farmers—80% of whom are women—in organic techniques, composting and the production of natural pesticides. The course lasts for four years and is delivered locally on farms. Each group is given a water tank with instructions on how to make additional ones. In addition, the project provides female goats and the women decide amongst themselves who should be the first to receive them. The offspring from these goats are then given to the next members in line.

Open field days are held regularly; they encourage the exchange of knowledge between farmers. In addition, a local resource person is appointed who helps deal with local problems.

Since 1993, some 60,000 families in four regions of Kenya have benefited from the activities of SACDEP. Diversification by farmers has improved food security and the women were actually able to donate nine tonnes of food during the 2011 famine.[134]

The Open field days are held on local farms and are also delivered by other Biovision partners. They generate enormous interest amongst the farming families, who often lack the knowledge required to cope with the effects of climate change and soil degradation. Farmers learn how to farm efficiently and ecologically; how to produce inputs such as fertilisers themselves; and how to dispense with expensive chemicals. This has allowed them to sustainably improve their living conditions.

The lack of any mechanisms for the dissemination of knowledge was also the reason why I founded the Biovision Foundation in 1998. Since then and as part of our Farmer Communication Programme, we have reached more than three million farmers in Kenya alone. This, however, is not enough. There is still much to do!

One of the priorities of SACDEP has been to encourage farmers to keep smaller animals and livestock.

P. 82ff. | Too much or too little water is an increasing problem for smallholders in Sub-Saharan Africa. Water tanks make it easier for farmers to survive periods of drought and a lack of water.

Mangoes are no longer crying

MERU, KENYA

At the end of 2011, mango farmers in the Meru District in Kenya sounded the alarm. "Mangoes were crying and falling off the trees," recalls Sakayo Murauki from the village Thuti. Every morning, mango farmers from the village of Thuti reported the same horror story: the ground was littered with beautiful mangoes from which juice oozed—it was as if the mangoes were crying. The inside of the fruit was alive with maggots.

At the time, Jane Biashara, a business adviser with Techno-Serve, was working with farmers in Meru County to increase mango production and market the fruit. To achieve this increase, farmers had been using large quantities of chemicals. Sakayo Murauki, for example, had been spraying his 520 mango trees with insecticide every two weeks, repeating the treatment eight times each season. All mango producers in Meru County had been persuaded to do the same. Yet large numbers of mangoes were now rotting.

"When the farmers rang me, I felt so powerless," reports Jane Biashara. The pressure was intense. "4,000 mango farmers were expecting a great deal from me," she recalls with obvious discomfort. Jane lost no time and started to do some research. She discovered that *icipe*, the International Centre of Insect Physiology and Ecology in Nairobi, was not only familiar with the problem, but had developed a solution. In 2003, *icipe* had identified a new species of fruit fly, which had originated in Sri Lanka. In Kenya, the fruit fly laid their eggs inside the mangoes where the maggots hatched. The fruits rotted and Kenyan mango farmers were excluded from the international fruit markets. For hundreds of thousands of families this was a catastrophe as they lost existential income from one day to the other. This fly quickly spread all over Africa because it did not have a natural enemy. Mangoes are among the most traded fruits internationally and are also important for local consumption.

icipe responded quickly and developed a range of innovative measures that in combination worked not only against the exotic species from Sri Lanka but also against the indigenous mango fruit fly. The system—Integrated Pest Managemet (IPM)—uses both biological methods and biopesticides, although the latter are only used where absolutely necessary. IPM protects the environment and reduces costs as mango farmers can manage with far fewer expensive chemicals.

The mango farmers of Meru were trained to use IPM and used the method from 2013. The success was almost immediate: infestation dropped quickly from 65% to an average of 15%.

"We are now producing top-quality mangoes and earning good money," Sakayo Murauki says. That is very important for him as he and his wife Jennifer earn most of their income from selling fruits, allowing them to finance a good education for their children. Veronice, their elder daughter is able to continue her studies to become an air traffic controller. Her younger sister is also planning to go to university on finishing secondary school.

The process was evaluated in 2013 and 2104, involving 828 mango producers. Of these, 694 used the IPM method, 134 continued to fight the fruit flies with insecticides. The yields, the costs for chemicals and other utilities, and the income from selling the fruits were compared. The IPM method performed significantly better: losses were 19% lower on average and income generated 48% higher.[135]

Right | Two kinds of parasitic wasps—natural enemies of the mango fruit fly—are being bred at the International Centre of Insect Physiology and Ecology (*icipe*) in Nairobi to be released in mango groves.

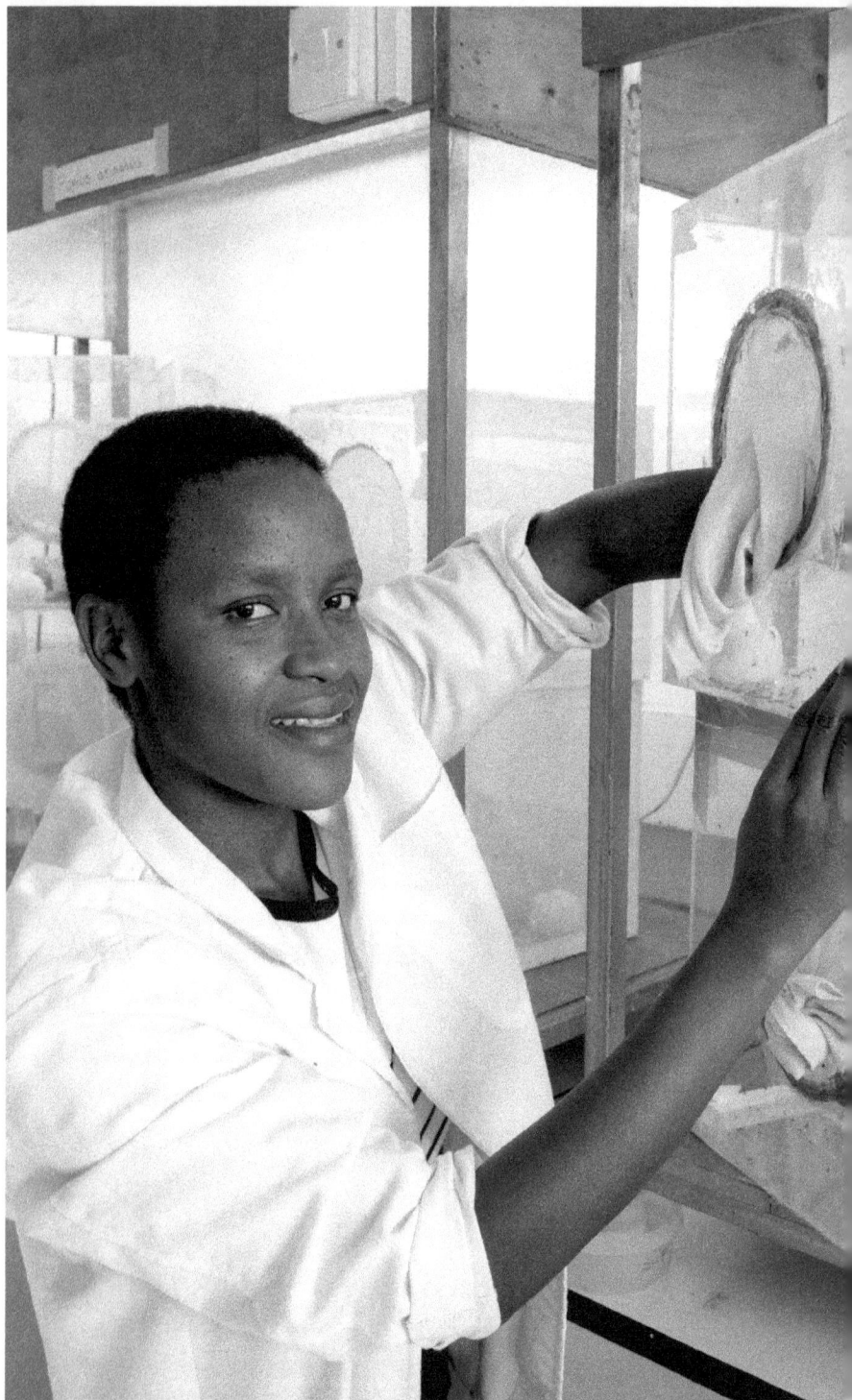

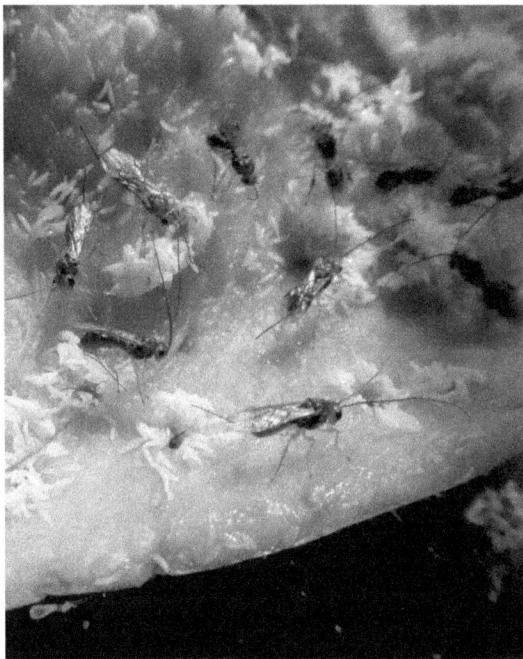

Left | Insect scientists at *icipe* have developed a series of combined measures with which mango fruit flies can be reduced and controlled in an environmentally friendly way.

Top right | One kind of the parasitic wasps places its eggs inside the eggs of the damaging fruit flies, another in their maggots. As soon as the wasp larvae hatch, they attack the brood of the flies and thus reduce the level of pests.

Bottom right | Without countermeasures the maggots of the flies grow inside the rotting fruits, and then get into the soil where they pupate.

Relief in Embu and Meru County (Kenya). After the fruit fly (*Bactrocera doralis*) imported from Sri Lanka caused great damage to yields, mango producers involved in the Biovision project were able to bring the problem under control thanks to IPM measures and could increase their income significantly.

Making a living with indigenous varieties

MERU, KENYA

It is a joy to look around their garden. The trees thriving on their 1.5-hectare plot provide shade, wood and fruit, and they protect the soil from erosion. Sheltered under the tree canopy are piles of compost and manure neatly covered with dried leaves. The various crops are all neatly planted.

"That was not always so," says Monica Gatobu with a smile. "Often harvests were poor; everything just grew wild and at random and yields were very modest," she recalls. Normally, they just about had enough food for themselves and their children, but sometimes not. "When that happened we had to rely on government food aid," says Monica. Today, Monica, Josef, their disabled son and the two children of their deceased daughter not only have enough food but they can earn money by selling their surplus produce.

Things changed when they attended a course in organic farming run by the Kenya Institute for Culture and Ecology (ICE). ICE is committed to maintaining local traditions, preserving and adapting farming methods and protecting the environment (see also "Marimanti, Kenya: The holy mountain is turning green again"). ICE pays particular attention to indigenous varieties of vegetables, cereals and fruits. Joseph Gatobu thinks that this approach has many advantages. "Our traditional varieties taste good and are healthy. They are easier and cheaper to grow as we don't have to add chemicals," he explains and stresses that farmers can produce their own seeds and seedlings from local varieties. This is not the case with modern hybrids, for which they are reliant on seed suppliers. "The indigenous plants also require less water and so are more resistant to drought and disease," he says with conviction.

The old varieties are also popular on the market. Monica says that in the past such varieties were both common and popular but with the passage of time many were forgotten as you could only buy the modern varieties in town. Demand continues to rise for these neglected fruits and vegetables thanks to word-of-mouth recommendations. "Customers will even buy their bananas or sweet potatoes direct from the farm," says Monica with quiet satisfaction. She reckons that she earns about 5,000 Kenyan shillings per month (about 55 Swiss francs) from these sales.[136]

The combination of traditional knowledge and modern organic cultivation methods can improve the self-sufficiency of the rural population. Old, indigenous crop species and fruits are well adapted to the local conditions. They are usually more resilient against the consequences of climate change and more drought resistant than modern hybrid species.

In a project supported by Biovision, Sabella Kian'a and her farmer group were trained to breed and multiply local crops. The farmers can generate income with the sale of these crops and their seeds.

Women carry the burden of responsibility

Women play a key role in small-scale agriculture in East Africa. Despite this, society continues to discriminate against them, preventing them from fulfilling their potential. Empowering these women would not only improve their well-being but also provide an enormous boost to the economy.

In East Africa, small-scale farms are heavily reliant on female labour and have always been so. The traditional division of labour makes women responsible for crop production, whereas men clear the land, prepare the soil and do the ploughing. In livestock farming it is women who look after the sheep, goats and hens, whereas men mainly tend the larger animals. But these women also have a myriad of other responsibilities, e.g. feeding the family, running the house, collecting firewood and water, buying and selling at markets, healthcare, and looking after the sick, children and elderly.

Women in East Africa already have a heavy workload. Moreover, the load is increasing as a growing number of small farms are now run entirely by women because their menfolk are living in towns seeking paid work. In addition, many women have to do paid work in order to supplement their meagre income.

Discrimination and challenges

Despite this major contribution, women are still marginalised and experience discrimination, for example in the following areas:

Land rights and ownership | In Africa, land is firmly in the hands of men. Traditionally, women own little land and so lack the associated rights. In those rare cases where they are the owners, they all too often end up with the poorer land. This discrimination against women is a major obstacle to efforts to increase productivity on small-scale farms.

Infrastructure | Inadequate infrastructure in rural areas makes it more difficult to improve the incomes of farmers. For example, poor roads, long distances and high transport costs hamper access to agricultural inputs, advice and markets. In addition, it is not unusual for some produce items to perish when transported from the farm to the market, thus reducing their value and the income generated.

Money and investment capital | Generally speaking, women farmers do not exercise full control over the income they earn, but are frequently constrained to hand over all or part of it to their husbands. Similarly, women rarely have access to loans. Banks are in any case reluctant to offer loans to family farms because they consider the risks too high. Women farmers without land rights and thus no collateral have even less chance of getting a loan. Without access to start-up funding, however, progress and innovation on small farms are unlikely.

Education and access to information | Although women are extremely skilled in a very wide range of areas, they miss out badly when it comes to education. If money is short, families keep the boys in school, but the girls are taken out early and put to work on the farm. When they are older, this makes it harder for women to run a business, interact with officials, attend training sessions or obtain the latest market data and information on technical innovations.

Health | Women in Africa have poor access to adequate healthcare and are more likely to be affected by infectious diseases, such as cholera, typhoid and HIV. This affects women in two ways: firstly as patients and secondly as those caring for the sick. The result, apart from the considerable suffering, is physical and mental strain together with a significant loss of productivity in agriculture.

Strengthen the pillars of society

Because of the key role played by African women in both the economy and society as a whole, they are often at the center of project work by organisations such as the Biovision Foundation. Unless women are included and given targeted support at all levels, it will not be possible to improve food security and health, end poverty, and encourage sustainable development in rural areas.

Full empowerment of women in East Africa would make a significant contribution to the economies of these countries. However, deeply entrenched traditional attitudes and policy failures mean that this is likely to be a protracted process.[137]

Mountain carrots

TOWELO, TANZANIA

Motorcycles are big business in Africa. Few can afford to buy a car for use as a taxi, but many can manage a *piki-piki,* the Swahili word for a motorcycle taxi. This trend is also evident amongst upland farmers in the Tanzanian village of Towelo, some 600 metres above the district capital of Morogoro in the Uluguru Mountains.

The village is home to 20-year-old Moses Paulini, who lives with his parents and three sisters. Their life on the mountain is difficult. The plants growing on the steep slopes are at the mercy of nature and the smallholders increasingly have to cope with the unpredictable effects of climate change.

In 2010, Pius Paulini—Moses' father—and others in his farmer group were trained in organic farming. The course was run one day a week by an adviser from Sustainable Agriculture Tanzania (SAT). The farmers learned how to cultivate the steep terraces to prevent erosion, how to make compost and plant-based liquid fertilisers and how to use biological methods of pest control.

"I previously used chemical fertilisers," recalls Pius. "They were expensive and eventually leached the soil. Yields were poor." At that time, his land only produced one or two pepper crops per season, but two years after the switch to organic, that number had increased to three or four. On completion of the course, Pius decided to grow organic carrots. They taste really good and are a runaway success in the town's market. Today, he sells 1,200 kg of carrots each season, which brings in more than 500 Swiss francs per year for the family.

Fortuitously for the family, Moses failed his school exams in 2013 and so father and son took a chance and started a joint enterprise: Moses became a *piki-piki* rider with his own machine—after his father invested the equivalent of 500 Swiss francs in a second-hand motorcycle for his son. The taxi business did well from the start and the young man regained his confidence. Since then, he has earned about 13 Swiss francs per day—8 of which he gives to his father. The residents of Towelo have also benefited; the *piki-piki* service reduces the time it takes to transport their heavy produce to the market in Morogoro.

All's well that ends well then? Perhaps not for Pius Paulini. Father and son have already come to a new agreement. "Moses wants to return to school and train as a mechanic at college. He wants to fund the cost of the training himself," smiles Pius proudly, but adds that his college fees would come from the 8 Swiss francs that he previously handed over to his father.[138]

Banking fields to protect them from erosion is an important improvement for the farmers on the steep hills of the Uluguru Mountains in Tanzania. They learn to improve their depleted soils with compost, manure and plant-based liquid fertiliser produced themselves. The new organic cultivation methods hardly cost any money compared to chemical fertilisers, improve yields significantly and soil fertility is increased sustainably.

Using biochar to protect the climate and soils

Coffee growing creates a waste disposal problem. The production of 1 tonne of green coffee leaves behind about 1.8 t of pulp. Pulp is a slightly acidic substance that is difficult to compost and cannot be used as cattle fodder or fuel. On the other hand, the pulp does contain 53 g of potassium per 1 kg of dry substance. This potassium was originally in the soil, but was extracted by the plant during the growing process.

A pyrolysis plant developed by the Swiss Ecological Centre in Langenbruck converts this waste product into a valuable raw material. Heat is applied to the waste, causing molecules to break down into smaller units. The end product is biochar that can then be spread on plantations. In this way, potassium is returned to the soil, and water and nutrient retention is improved. The process also produces gas and excess heat that can be converted into biofuel or electricity.[139]

A further benefit is that the overall atmospheric CO_2 is reduced if biochar is spread on the soil. This is because biochar can store vegetable carbon that would otherwise end up back in the atmosphere when the biomass rots.

The production of biochar from pyrolysis plants is one of the few opportunities to produce energy and at the same time reduce atmospheric CO_2. It has the potential to offset or even reverse the man-made increases in carbon in the atmosphere. Pyrolysis can be used to process millions of tonnes of organic materials, e.g. plant waste from agriculture as well as sewage sludge, wood shavings, driftwood, and biomass mixed with plastic waste and minerals. In principle, all hydrocarbons from wood to crude oil can be processed in this way so that the hydrogen is used for energy whilst the carbon is separated out and used to support plant growth. At the same time, biochar can aid the regeneration of degraded soils.[140]

Academic experts all agree that you would need 50 tonnes of biochar per hectare in order to increase yields—that is the equivalent of a full wheelbarrow of biochar per square metre. It would, therefore, require a huge financial and material outlay to apply that amount of biochar to fields. As a result, many farmers have dismissed the idea of using biochar to close the agricultural material cycles.

The Ithaka Institute has developed a method of root application. With this method, biochar is not applied evenly in large quantities to fields, but small quantities are applied to the root area (rhizosphere) of each plant. If this is done, one tonne of biochar per hectare is enough to cover the rhizosphere of each plant. In other words, a handful of biochar per plant is sufficient to achieve significant increases in yields.

Biochar is a delivery means for nutrients and before it can be used in the soil, (organic) nutrients such as cow urine need to be added. Compared with synthetic fertilisers, urine contains many more organic substances that stimulate microbial activity in the soil and probably also encourage plant growth.

In the next few decades, industrially produced biochar is likely to become one of the main raw materials of the bio-based economy. Simple inventions such as the Kon-Tiki kiln are democratising the production of biochar. Small-scale farmers anywhere in the world will be able to produce enough of their own high-quality biochar from waste materials and so regenerate the soil and increase yields.[141]

Right | Thanks to an extremely simple production technique, small-scale farmers in Nepal and elsewhere in the world have access to high-quality fertiliser made from biochar. Biochar is produced there from wood cuttings mixed with compost and cow urine. The mixture is then placed in the planting holes when the pumpkin seeds are sown. This has quadrupled pumpkin yields.

P. 112–113. | Prevention of nutrient loss should start in the cow shed. Instead of huge slurry pits, smaller collecting tanks for urine are built and filled with biochar. Periodically, farmers scoop out the urine-biochar substrate and apply it as a fertiliser.

Left | Biochar is produced from maize stubble using a Kon-Tiki kiln. The process is shown in in the fields immediately after the crop harvest in Terai, Nepal. Using local waste, it is possible to make one cubic metre of good biochar in a single afternoon. This produces a top-quality and inexpensive fertiliser.

Top right | Nutrient-rich biochar is placed in the furrows and covered with soil. This means that the delicate onion roots do not touch the substrate directly but gradually grow into it.

Bottom right | Stench-free thanks to biochar: the stalls are free from odours. Between one and 15 litres of biochar can be produced per cow per day.

Farmer Communication Programme *for East Africa*

The young agronomy student Veronica Wamiti may be much younger than her students from the farmer group in the village of Thayu in the Nyandarua District (Kenya), but she is accepted fully. The farmers soon realised that Veronica was an excellent teacher who prepared her lessons with meticulous attention to detail and was enthusiastic about passing on her knowledge.

Since mid-2013, Veronica has been making monthly visits to local farms to teach the assembled smallholders. It is the farmers themselves who choose the topics. They were particularly interested in learning about poultry rearing because it allowed them to earn cash by selling eggs and chickens. Farming families are very reliant on this income

In the break between the theory session on the different types of poultry rearing, feedstuffs and animal health and the practical session in the chicken coops, one of the farmers mentioned a previous attempt at keeping poultry. "I had ten hens and seven of them died," she explained looking somewhat chastened. She now knows that fresh water is very important for poultry. Veronica also explained that hens can be poisoned if empty pesticide containers are used for carrying water.

Veronica Wamiti looks after one of the advice centres that give farmers in rural Kenya access to education and training in ecological agriculture. Every year, some 30,000 farmers benefit from information and training courses on ecological farming. These centres are part of the *Farmer Communication Programme (FCP)*. The FCP uses a variety of media—newspaper, radio and the Internet—and personal advice to provide regular, specially adapted information and encourage an exchange of knowledge and experience between scientists and farmers. It disseminates practical, specialist knowledge that allows farmers to increase yields in cost-effective ways and achieve sustainable improvements in soil fertility.

An additional element of the FCP is *The Organic Farmer* (*TOF*), a newspaper for ecological agriculture targeted at small-scale farmers in Kenya. The Tanzanian version of *TOF* is called *Mkulima Mbunifu* (The Smart Farmer) and is produced monthly in Swahili. Some 250,000 Kenyan farmers read *TOF* and about 110,000 the Swahili version in Tanzania. In addition, up to 3.5 million Kenyans have access to *TOF* Radio that broadcasts two programmes per week.

The website *www.infonet-biovision.org* has a global audience and disseminates information on ecological farming, human and animal health care, environmentally friendly technologies and income generation. It is targeted at farmer groups as well as advisers working in agriculture and health. The website content is developed in association with scientists and local experts and adapted to local needs. Between January and December 2014 the site received a total of 533,000 visits, of which 127,700 were from Africa. Access by mobile phone is also on the increase—in Kenya, 75% of the population has a mobile phone.[142]

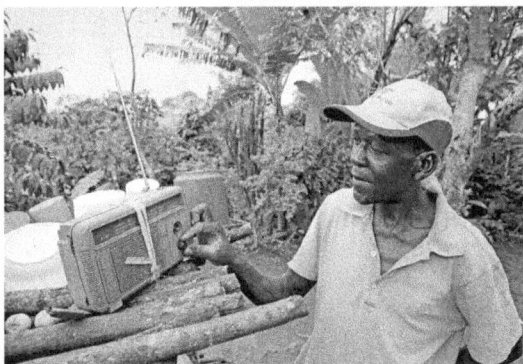

Biovision has developed a wide range of farmer information programmes that provide farmers with content of local relevance. The farmer magazine *The Organic Farmer* (*TOF*) in Kenya and *Mkulima Mbunifu* (The Smart Farmer) in Swahili in Tanzania gives farmers access to concrete, practical instruction on how to improve their yields using sustainable methods. In addition, *TOF* Radio broadcasts two programmes per week on ecological farming issues.

Practical training sessions allow Biovision to provide farmers in rural Kenya with information on ecological farming. In addition, agricultural advisers visit the smallholders in their villages and fields. The web platform *www.infonet-bio vision.org* — a sort of "Google for farmers" — provides concrete advice and instruction tailored to regional needs on ecological farming and other issues.

MURUNGARU LOCATION

4th February 2015
1. Official opening of the chief's
   by Hon. Stephen Kinyanjui Mb
2. Official opening of one classr
   Kambata primary school by H
3. Official opening of one cl
   in Hianyu primary school by H
4. Late birth registration has
   ongoing in the chief's office.
   exercise is still on.

Rice: Production boost thanks to the System of Rice Intensification

Rice is a staple food for over three billion people worldwide. It is predicted that there could be another billion rice eaters in Asia by 2050. For this reason, scientists are working to breed new varieties which promise higher yields.

The traditional remedy in this area—greater output from higher inputs—was fundamentally questioned by a new method of cultivation developed in the early 1980s by the French Jesuit priest and agronomist Henri de Laulanié. After many years of observation in field trials with small-scale farmers in Madagascar, he came up with the System of Rice Intensification (SRI); a system that requires less input but achieves greater output. SRI breaks with all established rules of wet rice cultivation. Firstly, seedlings are transplanted at the two-leaf stage (between 8 and 12 days old) instead of waiting for one month. Secondly, single seedlings are planted around 25 cm apart rather than planting them close together in bunches. With this method, seedlings do not compete for nutrients, space and sun, and develop stronger roots and more tillers. Thirdly, instead of continuously flooding fields to prevent weed growth, plants only receive the ideal amount of water and the soil is temporarily kept dry. This favors soil microbial development and reduces methane emissions. Since weeds have to be controlled manually using a mechanical hand tool, the soil is well aerated, thereby improving plant growth. Finally, organic manure and compost is used for fertilisation. Thanks to SRI, farmers in Madagascar were able to increase their yields from an average of two tons of rice per hectare to eight tons, with only one-tenth of the amount of seeds required.

Since 1997, Norman Uphoff and other scientists at Cornell University who had observed the success of SRI in Madagascar have been committed to spreading and documenting the method. With the support of farmers' organizations and NGOs, farmers around the globe have adapted SRI principles to their climate zones and local conditions, and have often been rewarded with record yields. Switching to SRI requires a lot of courage, especially in areas where the survival of families depends on the harvest. The method requires a lot of work and knowledge; for example, it is difficult for many small-scale farmers to irrigate the fields at the perfect moment. Nevertheless, 10 million small-scale farmers in over 55 countries in Asia, Africa and Latin America are now applying SRI. Authorities are already promoting the method in China and India.

"I think that SRI is something unprecedented, as very few previous innovations have shown such a huge productivity windfall. And just as surprising is the fact that we have been able to proceed on such an international scale with so little support and so much opposition," says Uphoff. Scientists from the International Rice Research Institute in the Philippines argue that the method is too labor-intensive and yield increases are not sufficiently verified. Seed and agrochemical companies are also not fond of a method that lures away clients by reducing the need for seeds, fertiliser and pesticides. Nonetheless, SRI is spreading rapidly.[143]

APPENDIX

Whilst working as Head of Research in many African countries and latterly as Director of *icipe,* the International Centre of Insect Physiology and Ecology[144] in Kenya, it became clear to me that that there was far too little communication between scientists and farmers. If we are to raise the living standards of rural populations, we first of all need to improve the dissemination of easily understood information on successful, affordable methods of cultivation. Secondly, we need to involve farmers more in the process of deciding what research is actually required. For that reason, I and likeminded friends set up Biovision in Switzerland in 1998 specifically to expand the exchange and transfer of knowledge and in general to encourage ecological thinking and action.

Since then, we have worked with partners in Africa to establish the Farmer Communication Programme. It uses a variety of media to disseminate information to farmers: *The Organic Farmer,* a magazine now published monthly in English and in Swahili, weekly radio broadcasts, an SMS service and the Infonet, a free-to-use website portal that displays not only important hints and tips on biological pest control in Africa but also information on many other topics.[145] The programme provides apps for mobile phones in areas without access to the Internet. In addition, we distribute CDs with offline versions of the online reference material. These CDs can now be found on the computers of many agricultural advisers, including government services. The information package is updated reg-

Diagram 6 | Map with areas in Africa where Biovision is active

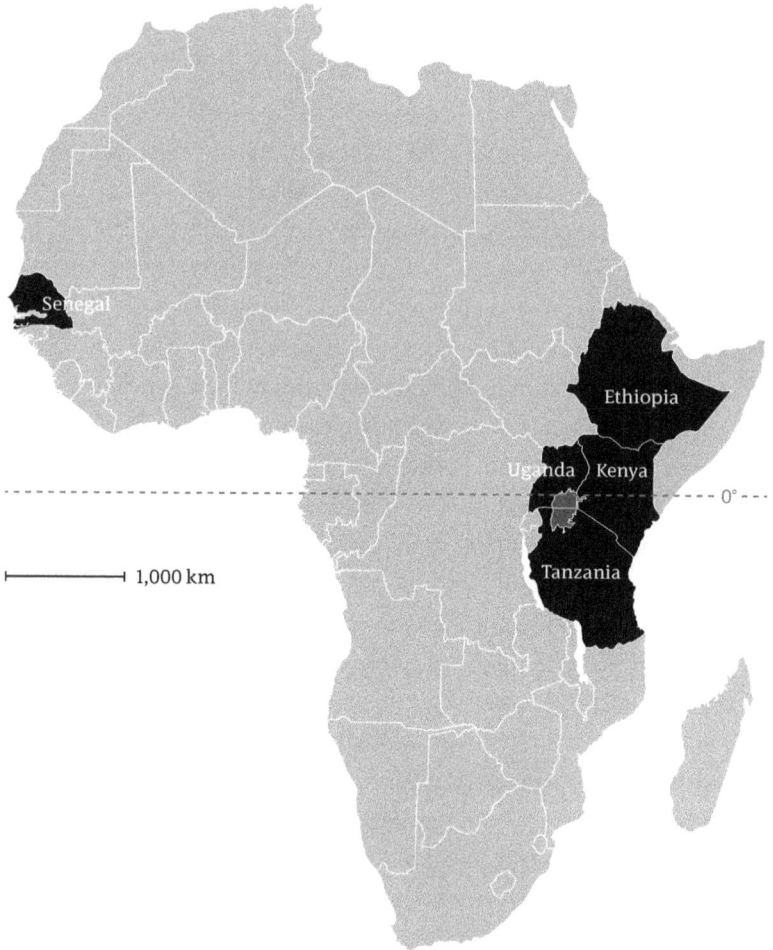

Senegal

Ethiopia

Uganda Kenya

Tanzania

0°

1,000 km

ularly with the latest content from the Infonet. In addition, we are supporting various local information centres where farmers can obtain advice. They are also home to agricultural advisers who visit farmer groups and give practical training. All these services are delivered by our African partners. The benefits of our interventions extend beyond food production. This is clear, for example, from our project on malaria prevention, where we are encouraging the use of biological measures to control harmful pests. Local people can largely keep the vector mosquitoes in check using natural measures. Such projects in the area of health also show that insect-borne diseases can be controlled without resorting to dangerous poisons such as DDT. They are also providing us with an opportunity to engage in international advocacy and argue for the replacement of such harmful poisons with biological measures that do not harm the environment.

Since 2011, we have been active internationally with a programme called Changing Course in Global Agriculture. A team from Biovision was present at the UN Conference on Sustainable Development in Rio in 2012, and through our efforts the final declaration expressly included a call for more sustainable agriculture! Also at Rio and following pressure from many organisations with similar objectives, the UN Committee on World Food Security in Rome was mandated to provide advice to countries wishing to bring about a change of course in favour of ecological methods of cultivation. Biovision is involved in testing this process, initially in two pilot countries—Senegal and Kenya—where it is also raising the awareness of local people to such issues and providing guidance and training if necessary. This work is particularly important because it allows the experience gained from our development projects to feed directly into the decision-making process of policymakers.

Such work requires complex planning tools, so Biovision works with the Millennium Institute (MI) in Washington und Geneva that I have headed since 2003. The MI has considerable experience in providing policy advice based on system dynamics modelling. Systemic thinking and planning is also crucial when it comes to the implementation of the UN Sustainable Development Goals (SDGs). We can only achieve sustainable solutions to the planet's most urgent problems if we think systemically.

Given that ecological thinking and actions are required at all levels, the MI and Biovision were active participants in the international process to develop Agenda 2030. Biovision, as the only Swiss NGO with general consultative status of the UN organisation ECOSOC (United Nations Economic and Social Council), worked hard during the drafting of the Sustainable Development Goals to ensure that those relating to food systems adopted an ecological approach—with success. Goal No. 2 "Zero Hunger" includes an explicit call for the promotion of healthy food worldwide and the development of more sustainable agriculture. This is very much in line with our motto "Business as usual is not an option". We desperately need a change in the course of global agriculture.

As Biovision has its registered office and roots in Switzerland, it is of course active in Switzerland. For many years, our interactive travelling exhibition CLEVER has been raising awareness of the need for sustainable consumption. It is both important and urgent to explain to residents of all ages that their personal patterns of consumption have an effect. What I take off or leave on the shelf in the shop has a significant impact on what goes on behind the scenes amongst producers. If I buy organic products, this equates to an increase in demand and so producers increase the production of sustainable items.

Similarly, at the political level we want to encourage dialogue between science, politics and civil society in Switzerland. The country has much to offer in the search for and implementation of solutions for a sustainable future. Our role, therefore, is global when it comes to the implementation of Agenda 2030. We will embrace work in developing countries and at home in Switzerland.

We can only provide healthy food for a global population that in future will rise to nine billion if we adopt an agroecological approach, display solidarity and responsibility, and make a commitment to sustainability. A world with enough food for all, produced by healthy people in a healthy environment—that is my vision. That is what Biovision stands for. However, it is also something for all of us. Please help! Thank you.

Notes

The following websites were accessed on 14 March, 2017.

1   For his commitment, Hans R. Herren was awarded the World Food Prize in 1995 with the justification that he had saved 20 million people from dying from starvation.

2   UN General Assembly: Agriculture development, food security and nutrition. Report by the Secretary-General, 2015.

3   Translator's Note: English version Wikipedia: https://en.wikipedia.org/wiki/Hunger.

4   Food and Agriculture Organization of the United National (FAO): The State of Food Insecurity in the World 2015. www.fao.org/hunger/key-messages/en.

5   Agriculture at a crossroads: Findings and recommendations for future farming, p.1. Translator's Note: English version www. globalagriculture.org/fileadmin/files/weltagrarbericht/EnglishBrochure/BrochureIAASTD_en_web_small.pdf.

6   Ibid., p.7.

7   UNO General Assembly: Agriculture development, food security and nutrition. Report of the Secretary-General, 2015.

8   Institution of Mechanical Engineers: Global food. Waste not, want not, 2013, p.2. www.imeche.org/policy-and-press/reports/detail/global-food-waste-not-want-not.

9   Verein foodwaste.ch: Foodwaste in der Schweiz. http://foodwaste.ch/was-ist-food-waste (German only).

10   www.biovision.ch/en/news/details/article/mehr-einsatz-gegen-food-waste-gefordert.

>   World Resources Institute. www.wri.org/news/2016/06/release-first-ever-global-standard-measure-food-loss-and-waste-introduced-international.

11   See Note 5, p. 20.

12   The Government Office for Science: Foresight: The Future of Food and Farming, Final Project Report, London 2011, p. 14.

13   Fleischkonsum 2015: 51,35 Kilogramm pro Person, 2016. www.schweizerfleisch.ch/medien/page/2016/fleischkonsum-2015-5135-kilogramm-pro-person.html (German only).

14   Jeder Deutsche isst im Jahr rund 60 kg Fleisch, 2015. www.ble.de/SharedDocs/Pressemitteilungen/DE/2015/150928-Fleisch.html (German only).

15   Bolis, Angela: Les Français ont de moins en moins d'appétit pour la viande, 2015. www.lemonde.fr/planete/article/2015/10/26/les-francais-ont-de-moins-en-moins-d-appetit-pour-la-viande_4797354_3244.html (French only).

16   Müller, Alexander/Sukhdev, Pavan/Miller, Dustin/Sharma, Kavita/Hussain, Salman: TEEB for Agriculture & Food. Towards a Global

Study on the Economics of Eco-Agri-Food Systems, 2015, p.4. http://doc.teebweb.org/wp-con tent/uploads/2013/08/Towards-TEE BAgFood_15May2015.pdf.

17 Bundesamt für Gesundheit BAG: Strategie Antibiotikaresistenzen Schweiz (StAR), Bern 2015, p. 11. www.bag.admin.ch/bag/de/home/ service/publikationen/broschue ren/publikationen-uebertragbare-krankheiten/strategie-anbitiotika resistenzen-schweiz.html. (German only).

18 See Note 5, p. 10.

19 Ibid., Graph p. 4.

20 iPES Food. International Panel of Experts on Sustainable Food Systems: From uniformity to diversity. A paradigm shift from industrial agriculture to diversified agroecological systems. Executive summary, 2016, p. 4. www.ipes-food.org/images/Re ports/UniformityToDiversity_ ExecSummary.pdf.

21 Deutscher Landwirtschaftsverlag: Wie nutzen die EU-Länder ihre Agrarflächen? In: agrarheute. com, 30. November 2008. www.agrarheute.com/news/nut zen-eu-laender-agrarflaechen accessed on 9 Dec. 2016 (German only).

22 See Note 5, p. 10.

23 UN General Assembly: Agriculture development, food security and nutrition Report of the Secretary-General, 2015.

24 Mo Ibrahim Foundation: Ibrahim Forum 2011. African Agriculture. Malnutrition. From Meeting Needs To Creating Wealth, Tunis, 2011, p. 20.

> Possible English version at http://static.moibrahimfounda tion.org/downloads/publications/ 2011/2011-facts-&-figures-african-agriculture-from-meeting-needs-to-creating-wealth.pdf.

25 Food and Agriculture Organization of the United Nations (FAO): Achieving food security in times of crisis. World Food Day, 16 Oct. 2009. www.fao.org/fileadmin/ templates/getinvolved/pdf/WFD_ 2009_leaflet-en_web.pdf.

26 See Note 5, p. 4.

27 Bundesamt für Statistik: Haushaltseinkommen und -ausgaben 2013. www.bfs.admin.ch/bfs/por tal/de/index/themen/20/02/blank/ key/einkommeno/niveau.html (German). www.bfs.admin.ch/bfs/en/home/ statistics/economic-social-situa tion-population/income-consump tion-wealth/household-budget/ household-expenditure.html (partially available in English).

28 Eurostat: Final consumption expenditure of households, by consumption purpose. http://ec.euro pa.eu/eurostat/tgm/table.do?tab= table&init=1&plugin=1&pcode=tsd pc520&language=en. Some English stats at http://ec. europa.eu/eurostat/web/products-datasets/-/TSDPC520.

29 See Note 5, p. 4.

30 Greenpeace: Agriculture at a Crossroads. Food for survival,

2009, p. 10. www.greenpeace.org/
international/en/publications/
reports/agriculture-at-a-cross-
roads-report.

31 Food and Agriculture Organization of the United Nations (FAO):
The State of Food Insecurity in the
World 2015. www.fao.org/hunger/
key-messages/en.

32 Neuhaus, Gabriela: Nahrung für
alle – oder wo ein Wille ist, gibt
es Wege. In: DEZA (Hrsg.): Das
DEZA-Magazin für Entwicklung
und Zusammenarbeit. Eine Welt,
H.1, March 2009, pp. 7–11 (German
only).

33 Weltbevölkerungszähler – Welt-
bevölkerungs-Statistik. www.um
rechnung.org/weltbevoelkerung-
aktuelle-momentane/weltbevoel
kerungs-zaehler.htm (Geman
only).

34 High Level Expert Forum: How to
feed the world 2050. The special
challenge für sub-saharan Africa.
Rome, 12-13 Oct. 2009. www.fao.
org/fileadmin/templates/wsfs/
docs/Issues_papers/HLEF2050_Af-
rica.pdf.

35 Harder, Werner: Die Landwirtschaft als Schlüsselsektor der Zukunft. In: Bundesamt für Umwelt
(Hrsg.): Umwelt. Zukunftsfaktor
Landwirtschaft, H. 2, Mai 2008,
pp. 10–11. www.bafu.admin.ch/
dam/bafu/de/dokumente/land
wirtschaft/magazin-umwelt/ma
gazin_umwelt_22008zukunftsfak
torlandwirtschaft.pdf.download.
pdf/magazin_umwelt_22008zu

kunftsfaktorlandwirtschaft.pdf
(German only).

36 Worldwatch Institute: World
Population, Agriculture, and
Malnutrition, 2004. www.world-
watch.org/node/554.

37 UNO General Assembly: Agricultural technology for development. Report of the Secretary-
General, 2015.

38 Worldwatch Institute: World
Population, Agriculture, and
Malnutrition, 2004. www.world-
watch.org/node/554.

39 Hofstetter, Pepo: Rezepte gegen
den Griff aufs fremde Land. In:
Alliance Sud (Hrsg.): Global. Glo-
balisierung und Nord/Süd-Poli-
tik. Welche Rezepte gegen den
Wettlauf um Land, Bern 2010.
www.alliancesud.ch/sites/de
fault/files/documents/import/
GLOBAL%2B%20Land%20Grabbing.
pdf (German only).

40 Mo Ibrahim Foundation: Ibrahim
Forum 2011. African Agriculture.
Malnutrition. From Meeting
Needs To Creating Wealth, Tunis
2011, p. 20.
English version at http://static.
moibrahimfoundation.org/down
loads/publications/2011/2011-facts-
&-figures-african-agriculture-
from-meeting-needs-to-creating-
wealth.pdf.

41 Land Matrix. www.landmatrix.
org/en.

42 Wikipedia: Bewässerungsfeld-
wirtschaft (irrigation farming).
https://de.wikipedia.org/wiki/

Bew%C3%A4sserungsfeldwirt
schaft (German only).

> General article on irrigation in
  English at https://en.wikipedia.
  org/wiki/Irrigation.

43 Agriculture at a Crossroads. International Assessment of Agricultural Knowledge, Science and
   Technology for Development
   (IAASTD): Summary for Decision
   Makers of the Global Report,
   2008, p. 5.

44 Ibid.

45 iPES Food. International Panel
   of Experts on Sustainable Food
   Systems: From uniformity to diversity. A paradigm shift from industrial agriculture to diversified
   agroecological systems. Executive
   summary, 2016, p. 4.
   www.ipes-food.org/images/Re
   ports/UniformityToDiversity_
   ExecSummary.pdf.

46 FAO: Agricultural Biodiversity,
   2008. www.fao.org/docrep/010/
   i0112e/i0112e00.htm.

47 Bundesministerium für wirt-
   schaftliche Zusammenarbeit und
   Entwicklung: Kartoffelvielfalt.
   Knollen für die Weltbevölkerung,
   2008. http://region-hannover.
   bund.net/fileadmin/bundgrup
   pen/bcmshannover/Nutzpflan
   zenvielfalt/Ausstellung_Nutz
   pflanzenvielfalt/Tafel_6_DIN_A_
   4_Kartoffelvielfalt.pdf (German
   only).

48 Klaus, Gregor: Wertvolle Sorten-
   vielfalt. Die Bedeutung der gene-
   tischen Ressourcen. In: Forum

Biodiversität Schweiz (Hrsg): Hotspot. Der Wert der Biodiversität,
H. 12, Bern 2005, p. 18. www.natur
wissenschaften.ch/uuid/6f1774c4-
9582-52bc-8d1a-c6e929c7214e
(German only).

49 Klaus, Gregor: Die Bewahrung des
   Unbekannten. In: Forum Biodiversität Schweiz (Hrsg): Hotspot.
   Die Erhaltung, H. 3, Bern 2001, p. 3.
   www.naturwissenschaften.ch/
   uuid/e2f9e237-115d-5ef1-b339-286
   dcce1f7d7 (German only).

50 Weltagrarbericht. Nachrichten:
   FAO-Bericht. Seltene Nutztierras-
   sen vom Aussterben bedroht.
   www.weltagrarbericht.de/aktu
   elles/nachrichten/news/de/31602.
   html (German version).
   www.globalagriculture.org/
   whats-new/news/news/en/31599.
   html (English version).

51 Scholz, M. et al.: Wilde Verwandte
   hilft Kulturgerste gegen Krank-
   heit, 2011. www.naturwissenschaf
   ten.ch/organisations/biodiversity/
   publications/informations_bio
   diversity_switzerland/search_de
   tails?id=468&_ga=1.110891206.2119
   533182.1485341364 (German only).

52 Häner, R./Schierscher, B./Kleijer,
   G./Rometsch, S./Holderegger, R.:
   Crop wild relatives conservation.
   In: Agrarforschung Schweiz
   16(06), 2009, pp. 204–209.
   www.agrarforschungschweiz.ch/
   archiv_11en.php?id_artikel=1481
   (Abstract only in English, report
   in German).

53 Federal Office for the Environment (FOEN): Threats. In: Biodiversity Monitoring Switzerland. www.biodiversitymonitoring.ch/en/background/biodiversitaet/threats.html.

54 UNO General Assembly: Agriculture development, food security and nutrition. Report of the Secretary-General, 2015.

55 iPES Food. International Panel of Experts on Sustainable Food Systems: From uniformity to diversity. A paradigm shift from industrial agriculture to diversified agroecological systems. Executive summary, 2016, p. 4. www.ipes-food.org/images/Reports/UniformityToDiversity_ExecSummary.pdf.

56 UNO General Assembly: Agriculture development, food security and nutrition. Report of the Secretary-General, 2015.

57 Woodcock, Ben A./Issac, Nicholas J.B./Bullock, James M. et al.: Impacts of neonicotinoid use on long-term population changes in wild bees in England, 2015. www.nature.com/articles/ncomms12459.

58 Stehle, Sebastian/Schulz, Ralf: Agricultural insecticides threaten surface waters at the global scale, 2015. www.pnas.org/content/112/18/5750.full.

59 Munz, Nicole/Leu, Christian/Wittmer, Irene: Pestizidmessungen in Fließgewässern. Schweizweite Auswertung. In: Aqua&Gas, H.11, 2012, pp. 32–41 (German only).

60 Part 4. Business as usual is not an option. In: Greenpeace (publisher): Agriculture at a Crossroads. Food for survival, Amsterdam 2009, p. 30. www.greenpeace.org/international/en/publications/reports/agriculture-at-a-cross roads-report.

61 iPES Food. International Panel of Experts on Sustainable Food Systems: From uniformity to diversity. A paradigm shift from industrial agriculture to diversified agroecological systems. Executive summary, 2016, p. 5. www.ipes-food.org/images/Reports/UniformityToDiversity_ExecSummary.pdf.

62 Sustainable Pulse: German Beer Industry in Shock over Glyphosate Contamination, 2016. http://sustainablepulse.com/2016/02/25/german-beer-industry-in-shock-over-probable-carcinogen-glyphosate-contamination/#.WInVEDFviUk.

63 Infoportal Glyphosat: Trinkwasserqualität und Glyphosat, Dezember 2012. English version at www.glyphosate.eu/drinking-water-quality-and-glyphosate?apl=N%3B.

64 www.monsanto-tribunal.org.

65 UNEP: Towards a Green Economy. Pathways to Sustainable Development and Poverty Eradication— A Synthesis for Policy Makers, 2011, p. 50. http://web.unep.org/greeneconomy/sites/unep.org.greeneconomy/files/publications/ger/GER_synthesis_en.pdf.

66 UNO General Assembly: Agriculture development, food security and nutrition. Report of the Secretary-General, 2015.

67 UNEP: Green economy, Agriculture. Investing in natural capital, 2011, p. 40. https://web.unep.org/greeneconomy/sites/unep.org.greeneconomy/files/field/image/2.0_agriculture.pdf.

68 Heinrich Böll Stiftung: Less hunger through more ecology. What can organic farming research contribute, Berlin 2011, p. 3. www.boell.de/sites/default/files/Less-hunger-through-more-ecology.pdf.

69 iPES Food. International Panel of Experts on Sustainable Food Systems: From uniformity to diversity. A paradigm shift from industrial agriculture to diversified agroecological systems. Executive summary, 2016, p. 3. www.ipes-food.org/images/Reports/UniformityToDiversity_ExecSummary.pdf.

70 IPCC: Climate Change 2014. Synthesis Report. Summary for Policymakers, November 2014, p.9. www.ipcc.ch/report/ar5/syr.

71 Ibid., Graph, p. 32.

72 Wasdell, David: Climate Dynamics. Facing the Harsh Realities of Now. Climate Sensitivity, Target Temperature & the Carbon Budget. Guidelines for Strategic Action, August 2015. www.apollo-gaia.org/Harsh%20Realities.pdf.

73 Wiki. Bildungsserver: Klimawandel. Klimaänderungen in Ostafrika. http://wiki.bildungsserver.de/klimawandel/index.php/Klima%C3%A4nderungen_in_Ostafrika (German only).

74 Deonrarain, Bhavna: 8 Beispiele, wie sich der Klimawandel schon jetzt auf Afrika auswirkt, Dezember 2014. http://350.org/de/8-beispiele-wie-sich-der-klimawandel-schon-jetzt-auf-afrika-auswirkt (German only).

75 Wiki. Bildungsserver: Klimawandel. Klimaänderungen in Afrika. http://wiki.bildungsserver.de/klimawandel/index.php/Klima%C3%A4nderungen_in_Afrika (German only).

76 See Note 74.

77 World Bank Climate Change Strategy for Africa Calls for Adaptation, Mitigation and Additional Financing, November 2010. http://web.worldbank.org/WBSITE/EXTERNAL/COUNTRIES/AFRICAEXT/0,,contentMDK:22777785~menuPK:2246551~pagePK:2865106~piPK:2865128~theSitePK:258644,00.html.

78 EXILE Kulturkoordination e.V.: Klimawandel und seine Auswirkungen in Afrika. www.gesichter-afrikas.de/klima/klimawandel.html (German only).

79 Climate Change and Environmental Risk Atlas 2015. http://maplecroft.com/portfolio/new-analysis/2014/10/29/climate-change-and-lack-food-security-multiply-risks-conflict-and-civil-unrest-32-countries-maplecroft.

80 Biovision: Newsletter. Agriculture in Kenya on trial. Which is better:

organic or conventional? August 2016. www.biovision.ch/filead min/pdf/e/services/downloads/ newsletter/RZ_Newsletter_NL41_ EN_web.pdf.

81 WWF: Living Planet. Report 2010. Summary, p. 18. http://d2ouvy59 podg6k.cloudfront.net/down loads/lpr_summary_booklet_fi nal_feb_2011.pdf.

> Wikipedia: Ecological Footprint. https://en.wikipedia.org/wiki/ Ecological_footprint.

> Valda, Andreas: Konfibrot ist belastender als warm duschen. In: Der Bund, 8.9.2016. www.derbund.ch/wirtschaft/stan dard/Konfibrot-ist-belastender- als-warm-duschen/story/25344181 (German only).

82 See Note 5, p. 22.

83 UNEP: Towards a Green Economy. Pathways to Sustainable Develop- ment and Poverty Eradication— A Synthesis for Policy Makers, 2011, p. 41. http://web.unep.org/ greeneconomy/sites/unep.org. greeneconomy/files/publications/ ger/GER_synthesis_en.pdf.

84 Greenpeace: Agriculture at a Crossroads. Food for survival, 2009, p.19. www.greenpeace.org/ international/en/publications/ reports/agriculture-at-a-cross roads-report.

85 Schweizerischer Bauernverband: Der Platz der Landwirtschaft in der Wirtschaftslandschaft Schweiz. www.sbv-usp.ch/filead min/user_upload/bauernverband/ Taetigkeit/Argumente/03_Land

wirtschaft_in_der_Wirtschaft.pdf (German only).

86 Mo Ibrahim Foundation: Ibrahim Forum 2011. African Agriculture. Malnutrition. From Meeting Needs To Creating Wealth, Tunis 2011, p.12. English version at http://static.moibrahimfounda tion.org/downloads/publications/ 2011/2011-facts-&-figures-african- agriculture-from-meeting-needs- to-creating-wealth.pdf.

87 UN General Assembly: Agricul- ture development, food security and nutrition. Report of the Secretary-General, 2015.

88 Müller, Alexander/Sukhdev, Pavan/Miller, Dustin/Sharma, Kavita/Hussain, Salman: TEEB for Agriculture & Food. Towards a Global Study on the Economics of Eco-Agri-Food Systems. 2015, p.16. http://doc.teebweb.org/wp-con tent/uploads/2013/08/Towards- TEEBAgFood_15May2015.pdf.

89 Vock, Christian: Was kosten Le- bensmittel wirklich? Mai 2015. http://web.de/magazine/gesund heit/kosten-lebensmittel-306384 36 (German only).

90 Mo Ibrahim Foundation: Ibrahim Forum 2011. African Agriculture. Malnutrition. From Meeting Needs To Creating Wealth, Tunis 2011, p.32. English version at http://static.moibrahimfounda tion.org/downloads/publica tions/2011/2011-facts-&-figures- african-agriculture-from-meet ing-needs-to-creating-wealth.pdf.

91 Ibid.

>   World Food Programme: Hunger weltweit – Zahlen und Fakten, 2016. http://de.wfp.org/hunger/ hunger-statistik (German only).

92 Niggli, Urs/Forschungsinstitut für Biologischen Landbau (FiBL): Biolandbau, Gentechnik, Welternährung. A response to an interview with Nina Fedoroff in the NZZ on Sunday, 26 February 2012. www.fibl.org/fileadmin/ documents/de/news/2012/niggli-2012-replik-fedoroff.pdf (German only).

>   iPES Food. International Panel of Experts on Sustainable Food Systems: From uniformity to diversity. A paradigm shift from industrial agriculture to diversified agroecological systems. Executive summary, 2016, p.10. www.ipes-food.org/images/Reports/Unifor mityToDiversity_ExecSummary. pdf.

>   Kniss, Andrew R./Savage, Steven D./Jabbour, Tanda: Commercial Crop Yields Reveal Strengths and Weaknesses for Organic Agriculture in the United States, August 2016. http://journals.plos.org/ plosone/article?id=10.1371/jour nal.pone.0161673.

93 Niggli, Urs/Forschungsinstitut für Biologischen Landbau (FiBL): Biolandbau, Gentechnik, Welternährung. A response to an interview with Nina Fedoroff in the NZZ on Sunday, 26 February 2012. www.fibl.org/fileadmin/ documents/de/news/2012/niggli-2012-replik-fedoroff.pdf (German only).

94 Biovision: Newsletter. Agriculture in Kenya on trial. Which is better: organic or conventional? August 2016. www.biovision.ch/filead min/pdf/e/services/downloads/ newsletter/RZ_Newsletter_NL41_ EN_web.pdf.

95 UNEP: Green economy, Agriculture. Investing in natural capital, 2011, pp. 48–49. http://web.unep. org/greeneconomy/sites/unep. org.greeneconomy/files/field/ image/2.0_agriculture.pdf.

96 Forschungsinstitut für Biologischen Landbau (FiBL)/IFOAM— Organics International: The World of Organic Agriculture. Statistics & Emerging Trends 2016. www.organic-world.net/year book/yearbook-2016.html.

97 UN General Assembly: Agriculture development, food security and nutrition. Report of the Secretary-General, 2015.

98 UNEP: Green economy, Agriculture. Investing in natural capital, 2011, p. 55. http://web.unep.org/ greeneconomy/sites/unep.org. greeneconomy/files/field/image/ 2.0_agriculture.pdf.

99 Ibid., p. 60.

100 Forschungsinstitut für Biologischen Landbau (FiBL): Biobauern produzieren am effizientesten und erst noch sehr naturschonend, 22.8.2000. www.fibl.org/de/ medien/medienarchiv/medien-archivoo/medienmitteilungoo/

article/biobauern-produzieren-am-effizientesten-und-erst-noch-sehr-naturschonend.html (German only).

101 The Future of Food and Farming: Final Project Report. The Government Office for Science, London 2011, p. 29. www.gov.uk/government/uploads/system/uploads/attachment_data/file/288329/11-546-future-of-food-and-farming-report.pdf.

102 Northeast Organic Farming Association/Massachusetts NOF: Soil Carbon restoration. Can Biology do the job? 2015, p. 4. www.nofamass.org/sites/default/files/2015_White_Paper_web.pdf.

103 Ibid., p. 12.

104 Ibid., p. 9.

105 Ibid., p. 3.

106 Contribution de l'agriculture à la lutte contre le changement climatique. Lancement d'un projet de recherché international. Le »4 pour 1 000«. http://agriculture.gouv.fr/contribution-de-lagriculture-la-lutte-contre-le-changement-climatique-lancement-dun-projet-de (French only).

> COP21. "4 pour 1 000" – un programme de recherche international sur la séquestration du carbone dans les sols. http://agriculture.gouv.fr/cop21-4-pour-1000-un-programme-de-recherche-international-sur-la-sequestration-du-carbone-dans-les (French only).

> 4 pour 1000: Les sols pour la sécurité alimentaire et le climat 4 per

1000. Soils for food security and climate. http://4p1000.org/understand.

107 Forschungsinstitut für Biologischen Landbau (FiBL): Globale Analyse: Biolandbau reichert Kohlenstoff im Boden an, 16.10. 2012. www.fibl.org/de/medien/medienarchiv/medienarchiv12/medienmitteilung12/article/globale-analyse-biolandbau-reichert-kohlenstoff-im-boden-an.html (German only).

108 Lindenthal, Dr. T./Markut, Mag. T./Hörtenbuber, DIS./Rudolph, DIG.: Warum Bio dem Klima gut tut. In: Bio Austria, H. 2, 2010. www.fibl.org/fileadmin/documents/de/oesterreich/arbeitsschwerpunkte/Klima/klima_bio austria_1005_01.pdf (German only).

109 BLW: Die Ziele der Agrarpolitik 2014–2017 können erreicht werden, 16.6.2015. www.admin.ch/gov/de/start/dokumentation/medienmitteilungen.msg-id-57692.html (German only).

110 UNEP: Green economy, Agriculture. Investing in natural capital, 2011, p. 36. http://web.unep.org/greeneconomy/sites/unep.org.greeneconomy/files/field/image/2.0_agriculture.pdf.

111 Wikipedia: Fairer Handel. https://de.wikipedia.org/wiki/Fairer_Handel. English: https://en.wikipedia.org/wiki/Fair_trade.

112 UN General Assembly: Agriculture development, food security

and nutrition. Report of the Secretary-General, 2015.

113 Gurian-Sherman, Doug: The Root of the Rootworm Problem. What a Tiny Beetle Can Tell Us About Our Broken Agricultural System, August 2016. http://civileats.com/2016/08/25/the-root-of-the-rootworm-problem-what-a-tiny-beetle-can-tell-us-about-our-broken-agricultural-system.

114 See Note 5, p. 7.

115 Hilbeck, Angelika/Herren, Hans: Millions Spent, No One Served. Who Is to Blame for the Failure of GMO Golden Rice? August 2016. www.independentsciencenews.org/health/millions-spent-who-is-to-blame-failure-gmo-golden-rice.

116 Vasileva, Adelina: Biofortification wins 2016 World Food Prize 10 July 2016. www.eatglobe.com/news/food/2144-biofortification-wins-2016-world-food-prize.html.

117 UNEP: Green economy, Agriculture. Investing in natural capital, 2011, p. 61. http://web.unep.org/greeneconomy/sites/unep.org.greeneconomy/files/field/image/2.0_agriculture.pdf.

118 Ibid., p. 58.

119 Created with ECOSPEED Private. www.ecospeed.ch/welcome/en.

120 Jungbluth, Niels/Eggenberger, Simon/Keller, Regula: Ökoprofil von Ernährungsstilen. ESU-services Ltd. Commissioned by WWF Switzerland, Zurich 2015. https://assets.wwf.ch/downloads/2016_03_14_studie_oekoprofil_von_ernaehrungsstilen___esu_services.pdf (German only).

121 Lee, Felix: Fleischkonsum in China. Der Terminator steht auf Tofu. In: Die Zeit, 28. Juli 2016. www.zeit.de/wissen/umwelt/2016-06/fleischkonsum-china-regierung-regulierung (German only).

122 See Note 5, p. 10.

123 FAO: How to feed the World in 2050. Executive Summary. October 2009, p. 3. www.fao.org/fileadmin/templates/wsfs/docs/expert_paper/How_to_Feed_the_World_in_2050.pdf.

124 Mühlethaler, Beatrix: Treibstoffe aus Biomasse. Kein Durchstart mit neuen Treibstoffen. In: Umwelt. Naturgefahren. Prävention zahlt sich aus, H. 2, 2007, pp. 52–54. www.bafu.admin.ch/publikationen/publikation/00174/?lang=de (German only).

125 Klima ohne Grenzen: Detaillierte CO_2-Bilanz. http://klimaohnegrenzen.de/kompensieren/detaillierte-co2-bilanz#flug-berechnen (German only).

126 www.globalagriculture.org/index.php?id=2003.

127 iPES Food. International Panel of Experts on Sustainable Food Systems: From uniformity to diversity. A paradigm shift from industrial agriculture to diversified agroecological systems. Executive summary, 2016, p. 15. www.ipes-food.org/images/Reports/UniformityToDiversity_ExecSummary.pdf.

128 UN General Assembly: Agriculture development, food security and nutrition. Report of the Secretary-General, 2015.

129 DEZA: 17 Ziele für nachhaltige Entwicklung, 2016. German version at www.eda.admin.ch/agenda2030/de/home.html. English version at www.eda.admin.ch/agenda2030/en/home.html.

130 Biovison: Newsletter, June 2014. www.biovision.ch/en/publications/newsletter.

131 Biovison: Newsletter, October 2014. www.biovision.ch/en/publications/newsletter. www.biovision.ch/fileadmin/pdf/d/services/downloads/newsletter/Kampagne_Push-Pull_Okt_2014_d.pdf. (German only).

> icipe, Push-Pull, www.push-pull.net.

> UN General Assembly, Agricultural technology for development. Report of the Secretary-General, 2015.

132 Ranking: Die ärmsten und die reichsten Länder, 8.7.2003. www.spiegel.de/wirtschaft/ranking-die-aermsten-und-die-reichsten-laender-a-256276.html (German only).

133 See Note 5.

134 Ibid.

135 Biovision: Newsletter, June 2015 and March 2016. www.biovision.ch/en/publications/newsletter.

136 Biovision: Newsletter, March 2015. www.biovision.ch/en/publications/newsletter.

137 Ibid.

138 Ibid.

139 Pulpa Pyro Peru: pflanzliche Abfälle werden zu wertvollen Ressourcen. www.oekozentrum.ch/291-0-Pulpa-Pyro-Peru.html (German only).

140 Die Zukunft ist klimapositiv! 14.3.2016. http://charnet.ch/2016/03/14/die-zukunft-ist-klimapositiv (German only).

141 www.ithaka-journal.net. English pages at www.ithaka-journal.net/?lang=en.

142 Biovision: Infonet-Biovision. www.biovision.ch/en/projects/international/infonet-biovision.

143 See Note 5.

144 www.icipe.org.

145 www.infonet-biovision.org.

List of photos and diagrams

About the author

Dr Hans Rudolf Herren, born in 1947 in Switzerland, is one of the world's leading scientists in the field of biological pest control. He lived and carried out research in Africa for 27 years. In the 1980s, he successfully controlled the mealybug threatening the cassava plant, one of Africa's staple foods. From 1994 to 2005 he ran *icipe,* the International Centre of Insect Physiology and Ecology, in Nairobi, Kenya.

icipe plays a central role in the management of pests, parasites and diseases in developing countries. Dr Herren has been awarded various prizes for his research on behalf of humanity, and in 1995 he was awarded the World Food Prize, the only Swiss recipient to date.

In 2013, he and his foundation Biovision were awarded the Right Livelihood Award (dubbed the "Alternative Nobel Prize"). Other awards include: One World Award 2010; World Food Prize 1995; Kilby Award 1995; Brandenberger Prize 2002; Tyler Prize 2003; Foreign Associate of the US Academy of Sciences 1999; and Member the Academy of Sciences for the Developing World (TWAS) 2005.

OTHER BOOKS IN THIS SERIES

rüffer & rub visionaries

Joachim° Ackva

**A bank account
for the earth**

Paperback
ISBN 978-3-906304-24-3

Humanity is facing major challenges. Achieving peace in a world spending more on armaments than even in the Cold War era. Imparting prosperity to the billions so far from it. Saving a world economy from drowning in debt. Preserving nature in an era in which the populations of those animals that constitute the bases of our ecosystems have been halved since 1970.

To overcome these challenges, Joachim° Ackva is calling upon each person on this planet to pay a sum equal to one thousandth of her or his net assets into the Planetary Bank Account, which is to be administered by the UN's Secretariat. These funds will go to decisively advance the achievement of the UN's Global Goals.

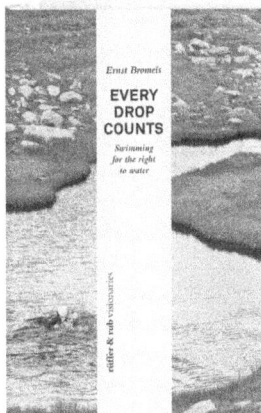

Ernst Bromeis

Every drop counts
*Swimming for the
right to water*

Paperback
ISBN 978-3-906304-23-6

Water is the basis for life on this planet. It is required by human beings, animals and the rest of nature. But this basis is becoming more and more endangered— by pollution, by global warming and by wasteful consumption in households. This is making water more and more valuable. That is why international corporations are purchasing rights to water. Switzerland is considering allowing hydraulic power plants to be sold to Chinese companies.

Ernst Bromeis' objective is to make us aware that water is not unlimited in availability. Large corporations are not to be allowed to exploit sources of groundwater in ways preventing human beings from having access to water, or forcing them to consume unclean water. To realize these objectives, Ernst Bromeis undertakes spectacular athletic deeds. Among these: in 2008, he swam across 200 lakes located in Switzerland's canton of Graubünden. In 2104, he swam the 1,247 kilometers of the Rhine, which starts in Lago di Dentro and ends in the North Sea.